"Shine on my voice so people hear it.
Lead me to speak the words of joy."

—Give Me The Faith
Jenny Berggren

Contents

Preface

Anyone listening to "Give Me The Faith" will encounter two bold requests placed within the song: "shine on my voice" and "lead me to speak." With those words, the singer recommits herself to the work of being a conduit. What does it mean to be a conduit—to use your own life to pass hope and joy and love along to another person?

When I listened to the track, and I did so often, I would always wonder about Jenny Berggren's tiny titan of a prayer nestled there within the verses. How were her requests answered and what did the fruit of those requests look like? I knew how it played out in my own life, but how did it materialize in the lives of others? I wanted to know, so I asked Anja and Jessi from The Jenny Source to help me find out.

We teamed up last October to start a project where we would ask fans one question: "How has Jenny Berggren's work and words influenced your life?" In response, fans shared personal stories from their own life experiences. The book you hold in your hands is the result. It is a sample of stories showing what can happen when a person uses their talent, skills, art—their entire life—as a conduit for a higher purpose. Stories that show what can happen when someone says, "Here I am. Send me."

Each story is told from a particular perspective and life circumstance. Some tell how Jenny's music—both with Ace of Base and her solo work—played a pivotal role in helping them during times of trial. Others tell how their concert experiences helped them create memories, build lasting friendships, and make longstanding dreams a reality. Still more tell how meeting Jenny brought joy, encouragement, a new perspective, and change into their lives.

While each piece of writing is unique, they all have one thing in common. Every story, whether stated or implied, holds the same request: *Sing Me Forward*. And that's what Jenny does for us, her fans. She sings us forward.

We think that a book honoring a singer for her work of being a conduit should be used as a conduit itself. A way to pass even more hope, joy, and love along to others—to you, the reader, in the form of stories. And to the Voi Project, in the form of funds.

The Voi Project is made up of individuals in Sweden and residents of Voi, Kenya. Together, they help provide orphaned children in the town of Voi with life essentials such as food, shelter, education, supplies, and more. It is also an organization that Jenny herself has supported for many years. All the profit from each book purchased goes to further the work in Voi.

Thank you for your support and thank you for reading.

—Sara West, on behalf of The Jenny Source.

Acknowledgement

Anja: During the last twenty-five years as a fan, I met incredible people from all over the world. I made new friends, I travelled a lot, and I heard many stories. Some of them made me smile, some of them brought me to tears. I am very happy that some of these stories found their way into this book, so thank you all for being a part of it and a part of my life.

Jessi: Getting emails and messages from fans to forward to Jenny, and meeting a lot of the wonderful fans around the world, I got to hear a lot of stories over the past more than twenty years. So when Sara presented her idea, I thought it was brilliant. Reading all the wonderful stories—and realizing the power of music and love people have—gave me goosebumps through every single story in this book.

I wrote my stories with different feelings. The first one is so unbelievable that I still cannot believe it myself. The second one just floated out of my hands when I started to write it, and when I finally knew where I wanted it to end. I'm grateful for the journey I was able to take over the past twenty-five years. I'm lucky for having met a lot of wonderful people and lifetime friends. I feel blessed doing things that I love and with people that mean a lot to me. You know who you are.

I want to thank Sara for the great idea and for the guidance she gave that lifted this project to another level. And for asking the right questions to picture the stories, so that everyone feels set right into the different scenes. I want to thank Anja for the past sixteen years of work and fun together. I want to thank all the Acers out there that have opened their hearts and let us take part in their stories, took us on their journeys, and shared intimate moments. Hope to meet every single one I haven't met so far at a future meet & greet.

I want to thank my mom for supporting all my projects since the early '90s. I want to thank Ace of Base, especially Jenny, for the sense they brought into my life. And I want to thank God who leads me the right way, even though I sometimes have hard times understanding the obstacles.

Sara: This endeavor started with a simple statement, "I don't know if this will work, but..." It continued with a response, "Go for it!" And ended here, at *Sing Me Forward*. Jessi and Anja's encouragement, knowledge, expertise, and support helped turn my little question into a big statement. You ladies rock! But you already knew that.

We asked our contributors to give freely of their time, talent, dedication, and heart—and they supplied it with enthusiasm. I know how hard you all worked and the difficulties you overcame. Like you, your stories shine. Thank you, natural superstars!

May this book about inspiration and influence spark a bit of the same within you, dear reader. I hope you will find yourself here within these words—and be moved forward in your own way.

A Bridge Over Time

by Anastasia K.

It's no secret that our teenage idols influence our future lives, values, and choices a lot. Ace of Base is probably the band every parent would like to see as their children's role model. If there's something one can learn from their songs, it's inner strength and independence, living in peace with oneself and the world, optimism, and the ability to notice little miracles in our daily lives. I can't say I've ever been a rebel, but listening to Ace of Base, I realized I don't even have to be a rebel to be cool.

I still remember when I started listening to their music. It was spring 2007 when I was fifteen. On the last day of the school year, I bought myself a present—an mp3 with Ace of Base's albums. I felt every one of them was a masterpiece, and they didn't deceive my expectations.

There was a period in my teenage life when I thought summer was one of the most boring things ever: friends are away, it's hot outside, nothing to feel excited about. But that May, I felt that from now on, everything is going to be different.

Listening to the music from my childhood suddenly made me look at my life with the eyes of the child I'd once been. I realized I had everything I dreamt about when I was little, and I just didn't have any reasons to feel sad or worried.

I can say their music helped me find a new source of inspiration—my own childhood—and it returned me to the happiness I thought I'd lost.

Anastasia visiting Kaliningrad to see Jenny in concert (2017)

ABOUT THE AUTHOR: Anastasia's a laid-back hedonist who lives in Estonia. Ace of Base motivated her to learn Nordic languages, and now she works as a translator. Her favorite songs are "Young And Proud" and "Pole Position."

A Secret in Listening

by Aldo Alvarado

I had never been interested in lyrics that I did not understand. I was sixteen and naive, but there was something in the beat of that particular style. Something so soothing in the color of those voices. From that moment, I wanted to know what every word meant. Ace of Base was the very first band singing in English to catch my attention. Without knowing who they were or where they were from, their music entered my senses where it has remained.

My resources were limited back then. I could access the local radio and television stations, but no cable or internet. Acquiring information about any artist was difficult for me. All I really knew was the name of the band and the titles of their singles. One day, while walking through a street bazaar in Mexico City, I found my first gem in this treasure chest. A compact disc with a bee on it. Although it had only one song, it came with many remixes. A few months went by and I never got tired of playing my disc every time the player was available. At that time, I shared a Discman with my two younger sisters before I got my own.

Time went on and destiny pushed me to make a huge decision: I moved to the United States. I am a man from a small, small Mexican village but Texas would become my new home for an undetermined length of time. I was eighteen years of age when that big change took place. Among the few things that I brought with me was, of course, my music. The language barrier was a fear, although it was not the worst because the surroundings and the new people were. There were so many people with different cultures and different points of view. I struggled to cope with it all. For several months, I faced discrimination and racism. And it made me push harder to learn English.

In a second-hand music shop, I found the second album. The style was quite different from the few tracks I knew from the first album, but I still loved it. And the translation of every song took off. I was lucky it came with the lyrics so I could read them on my own, and the more I understood the lyrics, the more I loved it. Not much later, I was able to purchase the previous album (not the U.S. version). It also included the lyrics, which made me really happy. The process was the same: a dictionary in hand, a pen, and paper.

As I fell deeper and deeper in love, I realized I liked the fact that Jenny participated much more on the second production. Before I saw the band, I could have sworn there was only one singer. My hearing was so uneducated that I could not distinguish between the two sisters' voices. This was a new ability that, little by little, came to me. Out of the three gems I owned, it was clear that my favorites were the recordings from album number two. An album which still plays perfectly with no skips. Surprising, considering all the times I listened to it.

A memory from 1998 still lingers, as if it were yesterday. I was walking past the music section in a store called Target with no plans to buy any music. Suddenly, and in a weird way, an item caught my attention from far away. Was it the colors? Was it because it looked like it was shining all by itself, as if everything else around it was blurred? I could not read the title since I have terrible eyesight. And the image projected by Ulf and the Berggrens was totally new. It was like slow motion. Me approaching the shelf to find the third album—an album I had not even the most remote idea existed. I don't think I slept that night because, needless to say, I took the CD home and listened to it over and over.

Sadly, the written lyrics were not part of the booklet and I was still way too poor in the language. I was eager to understand the songs and I was too shy to ask for help, but I did. I asked a high school friend to help me translate track six, which would become one of my favorite songs by Jenny. My ears allowed me to know that she was the lead voice in this cut, making me shiver each time I played it. I know my friend was annoyed after repeating the song so many times to figure out the lyrics.

Once I had access to the web, a whole new Acer-World opened up. And, using the speed of dial-up, I rushed to acquire anything I could find, absorbing like a sponge so much interesting information and songs I never knew existed, despite my mild dyslexia. There weren't any close friends with the same interests and admiration that I had for these Scandinavians—until I discovered the fan boards like Teenage Heaven. There, I had the opportunity to make acquaintances and friends, some I no longer have and many that have become an important part of my life.

I began to collect more and more material like singles from Europe, Asia, and South America. I was hooked on this Stockholm radio channel called "Mix Megapol." It used to keep me up late at night just so I could hear those singles making it big on that side of the planet. Then the Polaroid album surprised me! With no way to find it in Texas, I had to import it. Japan was the first edition I could put my hands on. At this point, I moved on from the idea of ever having Linn back. Her minimal participation in this production made me appreciate Jenny's work and vocal growth like I never did before. I moved past my desire to see her sister in a music video again, or anywhere. Although it has been nice to hear her voice in several songs that never made it to the official albums.

Jenny Cecilia Berggren, our Jenny. The one person on earth I can thank for being the reason I have friends in other cities and other countries. As close as my own dear Mexico and as far as Indonesia and Australia. Jenny's songs in her early career and up to today have become part of me with every word, every chord. I do not just love her fantastic mezzo-soprano voice, but also the magical effect it gives to each composition. I think of her as the only active member, but I think of her as so much more too. Jenny continued to sing for us. As if the love we feel for her energized her creativity to give us love back in the form of music.

My Story, her story, turned me into a different person, believe it or not. It helped me to conquer some fears (Some fears I thought helped me to live, but most of them kept me from living). Also, it helped me to believe in myself and to have a little bit of self-esteem, which I had lacked my entire life. I was the type of person who never wanted to meet new people, fearing rejection. I never liked crowded places and hated speaking in public even more. I would never have believed that I could meet fans from other cities in person and interact with them. Spending time in the same place, exchanging experiences, and having fun.

Oh, goodness, it was so hard to overcome my anxiety at my very first Acer Meeting. It was so hard to hold back my tears of happiness that finally rolled when I heard Jenny sing during a Skype chat just to us. Especially for us.

Music for the heart is what I enjoy—and music for the heart is what Jenny makes. Meeting her was, indeed, one of the greatest moments I've ever lived, and she changed that too. I never thought I would be so close to her, feeling her vibe, and seeing her perform live. I wish more people gave her music a chance. I would love for new generations to learn about her and learn to appreciate what her work is capable of. She has inspired me in many ways, and she has made my knowledge of music grow day after day.

Directly or indirectly, she has been a reason why I feel loved today and why I feel so much love to give as well. Music like Jenny's can really make a difference. It made a difference in me.

Music is not just the beats that make our bodies shake or the rhythms that make us want to dance. Music is not just a way to break the silence or a way to sing along. Music is much more than that.

My music journey has spanned more than two decades. My senses can now enjoy this art entirely because, besides just letting the record spin, there is more: there is a secret in listening.

Aldo showing his newly signed Flowers vinyl in Chicago (2017)

ABOUT THE AUTHOR: Aldo is a shy person by nature. He resides in Houston, Texas, USA and has done so since 1998, making it over half of his life. He has worked for the restaurant industry since age eighteen. Aldo enjoys listening to European music, especially from Italy and, of course, Sweden. (He can't get enough köttbullar with jam.) He is also passionate about cinematography, a field where he can be quite analytical. You can find him in just about any social media as @aceofbase01.

The Way to a Friend

by Leire Alonso Garzón

My name is Leire, the youngest of three siblings and the only girl. I grew up in Bilbao, Spain, and I was spontaneous and open with everyone when I was young. Upon reaching adolescence, I closed up a little. While my friends went out to meet guys, I stayed at home and listened to Ace of Base (who I discovered when I was ten, thanks to my brother). To date, not a single day has passed without listening to their music. Here is the story of how my life has been and how music has been my best friend, my companion, my therapy.

When I was sixteen, I met an attractive, handsome boy: blond, blue eyes, outgoing, and unafraid of rejection. Months passed and he showed interest in me. Our relationship started gradually and everything was great. He was attentive and caring.

At seventeen, I got pregnant. I decided to have the baby. And my mother, because of her beliefs, could not fathom the idea of having a child out of wedlock, so he and I married when I was seven months pregnant. Everything seemed to move fast, but at the same time, I was happy to have a family—even at my young age.

My husband came to live with me at my parents' house. I was eighteen when my son was born. Everything seemed to be going great. Gradually, my husband's attitude changed. I gained weight and he reminded me of it from time to time. He never changed a diaper or fed our son, or even gave him a kiss goodnight. My mother did not support me much since she grew up in a macho environment that taught her that the woman is in charge of the children. Time passed and the child grew, and the situation grew worse.

I no longer wanted be alone with my husband because I did not feel comfortable, so I tried to spend time with my friends to feel safe. These things were happening to me and I never told anyone. My way of venting was to put on my headphones and listen to songs like "Ravine," "Everytime It Rains," and "Never Gonna Say I'm Sorry." I identified with each song for different reasons.

For me it was always raining with a storm. And I wished that the person I married would love me in the same way I loved him. But it was not like that. "Everytime It Rains" helped me to vent many times.

"Ravine" is based on a tragic event, but I identified with it. It gave me the strength to continue on each day. It freed me to hear it. I cried, and even today, I still cry. I feel it close to me, as my consolation.

I thought the situation was happening because I provoked him. That it was not what he wanted and that's why he treated me like that. But I came to the conclusion that it is not my fault that he is that way, that I do not have to ask for forgiveness for anything. That I have to gather strength and continue forward because I have a child to take care of, and to give the best of myself so I can always be there for him. "Never Gonna Say I'm Sorry" pushed me forward, made me aware of reality. It will always be my favorite song, along with "Ravine," for its meaning.

October 31, 2005 was the happiest day of my life after the birth of my son. I went to meet my idols in Antwerpen. That day, all my worries disappeared for a few hours. I never thought that I would meet them. It was the first time I was going to see them since I learned about their existence in 1994.

It was an incredible experience. I stood in front of them and I did not know what to say. I gave everyone a bottle of wine. And I gave Jenny a little jacket and baby socks that my mother had made since Jenny had just given birth to her son. She loved the gifts. I keep the photos of that day as if they are gold. And when the concert time arrived, I was ecstatic. I danced and enjoyed it like never before.

I never thought that I would meet them. It was very special for me because everything that was happening around me in my personal life was so bad. This gave me strength, but I had no idea that things could get worse.

My life became unbearable. Psychological abuse occurred almost daily. My husband would come home from work and the first thing he would do was turn on a computer and show me photos of girls and say, "You see? These are women. Not like you. You're fat." (This insult haunts me still today.) Or at night, he would want to make love (if you can call it that…) and I did not want to, so he decided to throw me off the bed and leave me on the floor until I said yes. I did not say yes, so I slept on the floor.

I did not want to say anything to my parents out of fear and shame. Back then, I was young and was not really aware of the danger. He controlled everything I did: the money I spent, the clothes I wore…

I continued to take refuge in my son—and in the music. It was my way to disconnect from everything. But the day came when I decided to separate because I could not take it anymore.

That's when his threats and harassment began following me everywhere. My child, luckily, did not realize what was happening, except one day when he saw my husband grab my neck.

We separated, each making our own lives. He visited my house to see my son because I never wanted to keep them from each other, and I thought everything would start to get better. But it did not. And since he knew I was afraid of him, he took advantage of that. I thought I would not be able to denounce him for everything that had happened in the six years we were married. Then the moment came when I got tired of everything. I confronted him.

That's when he threatened me with a knife, pulled pepper spray, and pushed me against a car. I could not do anything but cry and do what he told me. I took the car and I somehow drove with him sitting beside me to a place where I knew I could find "my friends." And I use quotes because in certain situations, you realize who your true friends are.

In the end, I called the police. They came and took him away. He shouted out loud that he loved me. That is not loving a person. That is submitting, mistreating, and humiliating. Sometimes I think that if I had not reported him that day, I might not be here telling my story.

The only person who was there for me after what happened is my true husband, my true friend. My therapy to overcome everything was him and the music. Without the music, I do not know how things would have turned out. Ace of Base has indirectly helped me a lot.

And Jenny is a woman who I admire with all my soul. She is a strong woman, spiritual, hardworking, a role model. She is a believer and draws strength from God. I am not a believer but I draw strength from it.

Today, there are still issues with the father of my child. But I'm not afraid. I face it and do whatever it takes. No one is ever going to make me feel like that again. Unfortunately, there will be people in the same situation that I went through. Draw strength from wherever you can and act: for yourself, for your children. Do not wait. Do not let anyone make you feel worthless.

I thought it was my LUCKY LOVE, but it wasn't. I was LIVING IN DANGER, but finally, I saw THE SIGN, so I said to myself: "DON'T TURN AROUND." And now I have a BEAUTIFUL LIFE and I feel like a NATURAL SUPERSTAR.

I now live with my husband and my two kids. I enjoy life and give thanks for what I have—and for Ace of Base and Jenny. Thank you for being a part of my life since my childhood.

Leire meeting Jenny at a Love the 90s concert in Bilbao (2017)

ABOUT THE AUTHOR: Leire lives in Leioa, a town near Bilbao, Basque Country, Spain because she loves the sea and could never live far from it. She is happy and fun, but shy and observant with people who do not know her (but a good friend once you get to know her). She has a phobia of insects. As soon as a bee or wasp approaches her, she flies instead of running. But pets are another matter. She has a dog, two cats, and a turtle at home. Music has always been part of her life. Since she was small, she has loved to sing and dance. She also learned to play the guitar, although over the years she lost those skills. She always looks forward to the future with a smile. You can contact Leire on Facebook: Leire Garzon Alonso

Such a Dream: Taking a Walk in the Park

by Jessi Dieckow

I don't know how you guys think about certain birthdays, but turning thirty was not easy for me. The closer the day got, the older I felt. As if this date would change everything. People who know me know how little I like birthdays and New Year parties. It just doesn't make any sense to me why one should celebrate because yet another year is over. That's why I headed to Sweden with my best friend Anja for my thirtieth birthday. The plan was to have a nice time, visit some of Jenny's concerts, and just take it easy.

My birthday starts at midnight as Anja presents me with a small cake and a candle—and one of the most personal presents I ever got: a beautiful book with wishes and messages from a lot of friends and Acers around the world. So I cry myself through the first hours of my thirties.

Later that morning, I have just stepped out of the shower when my cell phone rings. "Secret number." This must be my mum, I think, so I mumble, "Hi!", then I hear "Hi, this is Jenny!"

I don't remember much of what I say, besides a whispering "hi" but I remember very well what she says. First, she wishes me a happy birthday then she asks me how I feel. With her ability to see into the hearts of other people, she obviously understands how uncomfortable I feel with that thirty. Then she says, "Don't worry, it is only important how old you feel. And don't forget, the best things happen after thirty-three. Look at Jesus." This makes me smile. She knows how to cheer people up.

Shortly after that, we say goodbye. We will meet in a couple of days and I am looking forward to it.

Anja later tells me that she had written to Jenny beforehand. Jenny had replied that she would prepare something, so we are both happy about that surprise call.

It's the last day of July. We get up at 6:00 a.m. to drive to Långedrag. We catch the ferry boat from there to Donsö where Jenny has a lecture planned. We get out of our car and see Jenny waving at us. She's taking the same ferry we are since the boats only run once an hour.

While waiting for the boat, we talk about how we are doing and agree that we all had a short night with too little rest. Jenny needs to make final preparations on the ferry boat for her lecture, so Anja and I sit by ourselves and get a little rest after our early morning drive.

Jenny gives her lecture at the church, and after it's over, we have to rush back to catch the boat to get to the other venue. We get on a street, not knowing it goes in circles and we lose time—until Jenny ends up guiding us back to the boat right on time.

There we are again. Back on the boat. Talking about my birthday and how happy I am to not have had a party this year either. I never had big parties since my birthday is in the middle of summer. As a kid, all the children were out on holiday. Now, all the adults are out on holiday.

Also I don't like to think about mortality, which is connected to birthdays and getting older. I have had this feeling since I was a teenager. While my friends were waiting for their sixteenth, eighteenth, and twenty-first birthdays to finally do all the forbidden things, I never felt like that. For me, it was rather a burden. I'm more of a pessimistic girl. Instead of looking forward to see how much time I still have to explore and make the best out of life, I rather look back and cry about the things I haven't accomplished yet.

Jenny tells me she wanted to plan something for my day to make it special, but she didn't have time. She smiles with a cheeky glimpse in her eyes as she mentions the surprise party she organized for her husband Jakob when he turned thirty. She asks if we are prepared for the evening in Götene. "I guess so," I say. She smiles her little secret smile and says, "I think you aren't." I make a funny face and all I can think of is, "What is that supposed to mean?" She laughs and tells us that she will put our names on the list for free entrance into the park. It is more than we could ask for.

On the walk back to our cars, she asks me what songs I know that she is performing. I start to name the ones that pop into my mind. I turn to ask Anja for help. Jenny smiles her secret smile again. "What about 'Bless The Broken Road'? You know that song." "I know that song but not that much since I haven't listened to it that many times so far," I say. "What about 'Give Me The Faith'? she asks. "Yes, 'Give Me The Faith' I know by heart. Why do you ask?" "You will see," she says with a grin.

We all walk back to our cars. I talk to Jenny before she gets into her car. Anja is waiting beside our car a few steps away. Before Jenny leaves, she says, "Have a look into the lyrics." Then she sings the line, "That God blessed the broken road that led me straight to you." Again, I look at her like she is one of the seven wonders of the world. We are going directly to Götene. How am I supposed to have a look into those lyrics, and what for...? I think. (Oh yes, I am that old. Cell phones do not yet have internet access.) Again, Jenny gives me a big smile and drives away...

"What did you tell Jenny?!" I ask Anja when I get into the car. She doesn't know a thing and looks at me with big eyes. I am so tense that I tell her about the whole situation using one loooong sentence without taking a breath. When I stop, we look at each other—silence—and start nodding at the same time: "No, she wouldn't do that ... Well, this is impossible .... No ... Well ... Hahaaaa."

And so we travel up to Götene for Jenny's next lecture. We enter the park with no problem, just as Jenny promised. This park is awesome, a real adventure land. They have pirate boats and boats on the water, floats, jumping pillows. Everything you would imagine on an adventure playground. I tell Anja that I would love to try all these things. Too bad I am too old for that.

We walk around looking for the little stage where Jenny is scheduled to hold her lecture. We are not sure if we have come to the right place or if we have mixed up something since Jenny is not in sight. Another band is on that little stage and this doesn't seem to be the right place for a lecture. I look up into the sky asking for a sign if this is right—and in that minute we hear an announcement that Jenny will start half an hour later on that little stage. So we go there to find some seats and prepare our equipment.

This lecture is shorter than others we have heard before. It is basically a good, short presentation of Jenny's book. We can hear her band doing a soundcheck in the background during the presentation, which makes it both special and funny. It is a great feeling being at this event since it is so different from all the previous lectures.

In the evening, Jenny and her band (Staffan Birgersson, Terese Fredenwall, and Simon Petrén) enter the big stage stage to start the concert. This is a real concert; no church gig, no Ace of Base concert but a concert of Jenny with her own songs and some covers. I love it—even as it starts raining. I use an umbrella to cover the cameras and a rain jacket during some parts of the show. We sing along, wave with the crowd, check the cameras, take pictures, and cheer to the music. Too bad there are seats so no one is standing up and grooving to the vibe of the music.

I had stopped thinking about those little hints Jenny gave me earlier—until she suddenly looks at me. She tells the crowd, "There is a woman in the audience sitting in the front row who just turned thirty this week." And she wants me to stand up. She laughs her heartfilled Jenny laugh. So I stand up.

She says I should go to the front of the stage.

My brain stops thinking. I hear her introducing our website—and then I am somehow on stage. She says that everyone has to sing "Happy Birthday" to me, so the audience has to join her. She even makes them stand up all together.

I feel like a queen … well not a queen: THE Queen.

They finish and Jenny introduces the next song, "Bless The Broken Road," and asks me if I want to sing with her. I tell her I want to, which is more a simple "Ja!" or something between a "Ja!" and a noise.

Terese smiles big at me and says, "Welcome to the band!" I laugh because this is the most amazing thing I have ever done. So we sing that song. The only song I don't know by heart. Ain't that funny?!

We finish singing and Jenny whispers to me, "That was good, wanna stay here for 'Here I Am' as well?" Of course I want to.

I remember hearing "Here I Am" for the first time at the Gothenburg Book Fair ten months ago: Anja, Katie, and I are standing there chatting with Jenny at the Libris book booth when she suddenly waves her cell phone in front of my eyes, "I have my new single with me. Do you wanna hear it? Do you have headphones?"

With one swift tug, I rip my headphones out of my backpack. Jenny plugs them into her phone, but when Anja and I try to share the headphones, Jenny shakes her head: "No, you have to take the time to listen carefully to that song. I want your opinion." So I put the headphones in my ears. And the song starts.

I want to remember as much as possible. Trying to memorize the lyrics and being surrounded by Jenny's new song in that busy book fair atmosphere is difficult. It feels like everything around me is speeding up. All the movement in the background is merging into one big swirl. And in that swirl, movement and overwhelming feelings.

I watch those three pairs of eyes staring at me. Anja and Katie are eager to share the same experience. And Jenny, I can see the expectations and concerns in her eyes. Analysing my reactions, trying to figure out what I must think about this song that is so important to her. When I start to bang my head to the powerful beat, I see Jenny laughing. I love the song and the energy.

I concentrate hard to remember the melody, but with all the impressions, it is almost impossible. Then I hear my later favorite line, "I'm the queen of confusion." I have to laugh because this reflection is so true. I pass my headphones to Anja. Jenny looks as if she wants to shake me to hear my final review. I try to hold my poker face and stretch my answer, but then I have to laugh: "Queen of confusion? Yeah, that fits," and I laugh again. "Here I Am" is special to me because of this experience.

So here I am on stage, the intro to "Here I Am" is playing, and I hear Jenny singing the first verse.

This is magic.

I see the audience clapping and, at the same time, I picture myself standing in the Libris booth. I accompany the others in the chorus and sing from the bottom of my heart. In fact, I sing more than the others because I have no idea who has which parts, so the chorus is mine. This feels so, so cool.

And it feels so natural being on stage with them. Funny enough, I am not nervous one single second. I just enjoy myself and, if needed, I can be there the rest of the show. But of course, after the song is finished and after a warm hug from Jenny, I climb down from the stage and go back to my seat. Anja smiles big at me and gives me a big hug when I return. I have no idea how Jenny guessed one of my inner dreams. I guess she is just gifted.

I check my camera and realize the battery has died. I missed the recording of the best moment of my life. I'm devastated, but at the same time, there is nothing I can do about it.

When the concert is over, we wait for the others to finish. Jenny signs copies of her books and the band packs their stuff together. Terese comes down for a visit and we talk about how I liked being on stage with them, and how much I enjoyed myself. "It was the best thing I have ever done," I say.

Not only had I just enjoyed a great concert by my favorite artist, I had experienced a great boat ride in the morning with a funny personal Jenny and been on stage with her singing two songs—and it felt like the most natural thing. I think about how my teenage me would have reacted if she had known this would happen fifteen years after. Had I known this would happen to the thirty-year-old me, teenage me would never have believed it. Staffan joins us in that minute, wishing me a happy birthday and giving me a birthday hug.

Jenny finishes her book signing and starts for the backstage area, but then she suddenly turns around and sees me. She runs over to us, gives me a massive hug, and tells me that it sounded good—and that she had so much fun. I tell her this was the coolest thing I have ever done and that this experience was amazing. She asks if we caught it on camera and I tell her that my camera must have gone off while I was on stage. "Oh no, I will ask Simon to get a copy for you from the footage they shot," she says. So Simon goes and ask for a tape, which I never got my hands on, sadly.

"Are you hungry?" Jenny asks. She has sandwiches backstage, so we should follow her. Terese, Staffan, and Simon are there already. Johanna, Jenny's sister-in-law, is there too. A very nice girl, just as nice as the others. We end up enjoying sandwiches and cakes backstage while laughing and making a competition by whistling with a bottle. Obviously, Swedes know a lot of crazy games with bottles.

The boys discover a stage in the back of the room, which is the little stage where Jenny was holding her lecture earlier. We're still sitting there talking and eating with the girls when we hear the guys moving around in the back. Terese and Johanna follow to see what is going on. After five minutes, Johanna comes back and says: "Wanna come and play? We have the whole park to ourselves."

The three of us jump up. Of course we want to! So Anja and I run outside and search for the others. I have a white jacket I need to take off, so I return to leave it backstage. I hear Jenny singing loudly as she's changing clothes. I get back to the playground and the others are already on the pirate ship, which is something like an obstacle run. Being not very flexible, I don't manage to make it to where the others are since I can't find a spot to enter. So I have to wait until they come back down again.

Suddenly, Jenny comes running out of the building to join us. We go into another funny "building" with a lot of holes … something like a labyrinth, which is especially funny when you are grown up and hit your head or your back all the time when it's dark outside. We crawl through a rabbit burrow, meeting each other and changing directions when we do.

We try the floats after that, which are basically fixed logs pulled along by ropes. I end up on a float with Terese and Johanna while Anja is teamed with Simon. You have to pull yourself forward with the ropes to the end and back. Each team wins one time. We are exhausted and our hands burn like fire since we have put all our energy into it. Then it is Jenny's turn against Staffan… We hear Jenny laughing all the way to the finish line.

We are done with that, so it is time to try the boats. I almost fall into the lake getting into one of the boats, but then I make it inside. I've never rowed before, so this is a big adventure. Anja and I are laughing so bad. We're rowing in circles and almost crash with the others.

Then we find a huge jumping pillow and try it. I'm jumping up and down, down and up. I lose my grip and, faster than I understand, I find myself in the sand right on my butt. And it hurts. I see Anja and Jenny standing in front of me pointing—and laughing so bad.

I laugh too and persuade them to join me, "Come on, this is so much fun!" and climb back on to that huge air-filled pillow. We jump up and down, down and up until we are all exhausted… So, we go inside to pack our stuff and leave the park. Jenny hugs us again and tells us what a great day she had.

This day is one of the best ones I've had too—and definitely my best birthday ever. It is so surreal that I can barely grasp it. When I woke up, I thought I would experience three "normal" gigs from Jenny. Instead, I had a fairy-tale day that included an on-stage performance. This was more than I ever dared to dream—and totally unexpected.

Looking back, it still feels out-of-this-world after all these years. In terms of birthdays, this was not only the coolest birthday I ever had but also the biggest. Since I have my birthday in July, usually all my friends are on holiday, so I never get to celebrate this big.

All these meetings and fun times I get to spend with Jenny are the reason why I have so much fun setting up meetings for fans together with Jenny. It fills me with joy to see all your happy faces on the pictures and read what a great time you all had when meeting her. And I know that by meeting with her fans, she puts a little light of Jenny spirit—her joy, fun, and heartiness—into every single person.

A birthday to remember: Jessi singing together on stage with Jenny

ABOUT THE AUTHOR: Jessi lives in Berlin, Germany, and is one part of the website team from The Jenny Source and co-founder of Aceisland. Having been an an Acer since 1993, she is living her dream by supporting Jenny and her fans by organizing meet & greet events around the world. If she isn't busy cutting videos and editing photos for the website, she can be found gardening, taking photographs, traveling or cuddling with her dog Odin. Being the impatient type, she gave up on her attempts to play instruments long ago, but she still owns a few. She would rather sing in a church choir, which she does every week. She is a workaholic, working in an investment management company as an Asset Manager, project leader, and coordinator for digital technology; she is always on the run. People love and hate her directness, which can hurt both parties sometimes. Her favorite official track is "Numb." Her favorite unreleased tracks are "Let You In" and "Wish You Were Mine."

Thoughts on Ravine

by David McKeown

Initially, I never cared much for "Ravine." Then Ace of Base performed it at the *World Music Awards*—with Jenny singing up front. This performance highlighted what was previously an album track to me. And it brought the song to life. The expression and passion from Jenny let us experience the situation relating to the story behind the song. This was the first time I would have seen Jenny as the main performer. She owned that stage and delivered a flawless performance for the show.

The track is sung with passion, but is also solemn at the same time. I still feel there is a happiness in the song. Even though it is a ballad, there is still a mellow beat. It has a chill-out rhythm and also chilling vocals. The song itself contains conflicting emotions that shouldn't perhaps work, but they do. Jenny delivers the song ever so effortlessly.

Although it has its own meaning, it can be translated into our everyday lives. For me, it's a song about strength, being strong enough to overcome any day-to-day issues within our personal lives. There is always light at the end of the tunnel. "I was meant to be here" and here I shall stay and achieve my goal.

Dave and David McKeown with Jenny in London (2018)

ABOUT THE AUTHOR: David Francis McKeown was born in a place called Bellshill in Scotland. He has been a fan of the band since "All That She Wants" was released in the UK in 1993. He started working within the Scottish bingo industry that same year, and has been working in the industry ever since. David was lucky enough to meet Jenny and other amazing Acers earlier this year in London.

Travelling in Time with Jenny

by Aleksandrs Elkins

No matter what happens today, tomorrow will be better. That is how I think. I am an optimistic and friendly guy from Riga who likes to travel, loves tennis (to watch and to play), and owns an adorable cat named Phoebe. I've never felt alone because I like spending my time with friends, or watching good movies, or reading good books with Phoebe by my side. It is never boring being me and seeing the colours of life. I always see the good in people and in the events that have happened to me, so it is no wonder that my favourite group is a band named Ace of Base that sings only positive things (Ok, maybe in ninety percent of their songs). I always believed that the future can bring only the light of the sun and happiness.

In the beginning of 2009, my main Master's degree in Mathematics and Statistics was almost finished. I had some good events like an Ace of Base concert in Riga in March—and then everything slipped away. Some personal issues, such as the accidental death of my grandmother in April of 2009 and burnout while writing my Master's thesis made life difficult in this period of my life. These personal events, along with the economic crisis, made it hard to stay positive. Somehow I needed to find an exit. I needed some kind of sanctuary and peace of mind because I was a little bit lost.

My country, Latvia, is a part of the Baltic States. During the global financial crisis, the Baltic States were among the countries that were the hardest hit. By December, the number of unemployed had more than tripled since the onset of the crisis, giving Latvia the highest rate of unemployment growth in the European Union. Early 2009 estimates predicted that the economy would contract around twelve percent in 2009, but even those gloomy forecasts turned out to be too optimistic as the economy contracted by nearly eighteen percent in the fourth quarter of 2009, showing almost no signs of recovery.

Many people went abroad in a desperate of search for work. There were almost no families unaffected by the trend of searching for work abroad. Everyone said that people needed to become more efficient, but how to do it? That was the big question.

I decided to continue my studies as a PhD student after successfully finishing my Master's degree because the economic situation in Latvia was bad. There was so much uncertainty that I decided to improve my chances to find a well-paying job in the future. And for that, I needed to get a good education and experience.

Then things got worse. Outside was the beginning of 2010, and the situation became darker and more delicate. Some colleagues at work complained about their level of living and the boss' undervaluation of their work every single day. They were uncertain about the future of my organisation and, more nationally, of my country. I was in a qualm. "What do I need to do now? What does the future bring for me?" The big strain at work doubled with the strain in my studies (preparing for international conferences and preparing for my exams). I had no time for rest. Only music could help me have some good added minutes to close my eyes and to step into a fantasy world.

In addition to the global changes around the world, my favourite band started to turn darker and have differences of opinion. Fans of the group heard a lot of rumours and opinions, speculations that affected the relationships between us. I also need to mention that the rumours and speculations really hurt me. Some close relationships between me and my friends from an Ace of Base Russian language forum were terminated when hard and bitter words were said. Even Britney later in 2011 sang about the end of the world. It is always hard for me to have uncertainty. I prefer to hear bad news over speculation.

Everything that was happening in Latvia and the world affected the mood of everyone. Only things that gave me strength in the past—favourite music from my youth and faithful friends—could help me survive these difficult times. My friends (including Acer friends) and I were trying to stay together and help each other.

Thanks to Ace of Base's lead singer Jenny Berggren and her album *My Story* that came out in 2010, I could find this solace that I was searching for. Her music made my mood more positive and provided mental comfort. Her voice, which I have listened to since childhood and believe, gave me power to look forward with hope that life will be better in the future. With help from my PhD studies colleague Slava Ruza, I bought a copy of Jenny's CD. He brought me a copy of Jenny's *My Story* he got in a music shop in Stockholm. It helped me find my way. And I managed to release myself from the dark mood to become free from the situation that I was in at that moment.

Times of crisis are the most convenient opportunities for studying and improving our qualifications. It takes a lot of time and zeal because working full time and studying is not easy. I needed to say no to a lot of invitations to celebrate something or to see friends because of the time limits. After work, I needed to go to the university for seminars or prepare for exams at home by myself. I found more solace from the dark mood in Latvia through my studies. I spent almost all my vacation time studying, preparing for my exams, and preparing for PhD conferences, so three years ran out quick.

I communicate with people in person or via the internet, but I should note that I almost excluded spending time together with anyone during my studies. Friends moved away because I devoted big parts of my weekends to study. Of course, there were some bonuses, like my PhD mate who worked in Sweden and got me *My Story* from a Swedish music store. It was like a ray of sunlight that improved the mood of my life. Another classmate brought *The Golden Ratio* from Germany.

Jenny Berggren's song "Dying To Stay Alive" gave me faith to understand that even with the way my life was organised at that time, I was still living a real life. It gave me a reminder that "to live" means everything that we do now. Lifestyles and routines change—and we need to adapt ourselves to this: "Now everything is for change/And nothing's ever too bizarre/This is a momentary range."

Another song from Jenny, "Give Me The Faith," gave me mental strength to concentrate on my studies and helped me not lose my friends during those years of not communicating as much as before: "And my excuse ain't good enough/You think you lost me as your friend/But I miss you too, and I need you/But I got so much to do/I wanna know why my priorities/Are seldom me and you..."

Years go forward very quick. I could not be bothered with travelling because of my studies and my financial situation. Nevertheless, news and pop music from Ace of Base and Jenny were always with me. Ace Thursdays and Jenny's activity gave me power to continue what I was doing and helped me feel better.

As always in this world, dark times pass by like a thunderstorm in summer. The general mood outside improved. Somehow, people began to be more positive and economic activity increased in Latvia. My personal life improved because my active study time ended and I had more free time that I could dedicate to my friends.

Surprisingly, it happened that I reunited with old pals from the fan page of the Russian fan club, and in autumn 2013, we came together to see Jenny's show in Berlin. It was my first big journey by plane since 2011 where I did not have to deal with studies or work. It had been about four years since I had met other Acers, for example, Julia or Jessica and Anja (last time was in Sweden in autumn of 2009 for church concerts) or with Oleg and Sergey (last time was during the Redefined concert in Moscow in spring of 2009).

Berlin met me with doubts. The first awkward moment was to meet Julia at the hotel in Berlin. We chose to stay at the same hotel. How to talk to a person that you know well but have not spoken to for some time in real life? Was she angry or not? What would her body language say? Would be she as nervous as I? However, seeing each other removed all doubts. Like the pause in communication had not existed at all.

We began to speak about Ace of Base's and Jenny's career, the songs, and what we were expecting from the show while walking in the city centre and climbing the TV tower at Alexanderplatz. Then we had a meeting with Anja and Jessica near the hotel. We had a walk together to the stadium, had a chance to talk with Jenny, and took a group photo. The girls organised an excellent meet & greet event with the possibility to ask Jenny questions, to get a special Berliner t-shirt, and to take home a "Lucky Love" CD single. Great thanks to Anja and Jessica for organising that meeting in Berlin.

The concert atmosphere got back to the '90s cool, but the organisation was not the best as I need to characterize the concert itself. But the feelings were amazing. The smoking people around us and some drunk people were shocking. And Jenny's performance at 3:00 a.m. was a little bit too late… BUT! (a big BUT) The atmosphere of Acers coming together, interacting with new people like Alan, Farkhod and Michael—and talking about my thesis that everyone was interested in was like magic. It was worth everything.

The journey to Berlin affected my life later by helping me answer questions about how I wanted to spend some parts of my free time and my vacation time. Meeting new people like Michael, Alan, Lily, Farkhod, Pavel, Kay, and others for the first time was inspiring. It gave me a strength to wish for more travelling and visiting more of Jenny's concerts in the future. It gave me the strength to be more patient at work for having the opportunity to travel.

After that show in Berlin, I had a conversation with Julia and Anastasia. We decided that we needed to attend another concert by Jenny the following year. It was a real need to be together while our favourite artist is on the stage, our favourite music is performed, and we have a vacation from our grey weekdays.

Somehow, it happened that I was not the only one who felt that need. Because the feeling in our souls, when you met people with common interests, when you have many themes to talk about, to compare your thoughts to others, is amazing. It's like feel-good "drunk" vibes. We need not only an Acer community discussion via the internet, but also times to meet each other in person.

Not so long ago, Alan from Poland appointed a new Acer Meeting (weekend gathering for fans with interesting activities) in August of 2014 in Poznań. Since that summer, we have had a nice tradition of spending some days together with our favourite music at shows with Jenny—in Riga (Latvia) in 2015, in Otepää (Estonia) in 2016, in Tula (Russia) in 2017, planning in Riga (Latvia) and Bonn (Germany) in 2018. No summer days without Jenny! No summer days without a vacation. I need both during summer to fill me with positive waves. We all need to have a rest!

This need gives us not only a chance to hear our favourite music again, but also to visit new places. We were all new visitors in Poznań, Tula, and Otepää. During the concerts, we were meeting and talking with new people who also love Jenny's music (like Maria in Kaliningrad).

New places are changing my vision of the world. New ideas, new experiences, other points of view on the same problems, exchanging experiences—it all helps me better understand other countries, different people, and to see more good in my own country. Sometimes, it even makes me be proud of Latvia. I have more respect for my country, for some opportunities that I have—to be allowed to have a chance to travel, to invite friends to my country. I change some visions of other countries too, for example, of Russia. We were not afraid to go after midnight from a show by car that was driven by a stranger because there was no taxi service. Or meeting friendly Serbian people during a trip to Serbia in 2014.

Places where Jenny is performing, we visit for some days. Not only to visit a concert, but to also see a city, visit tourist spots, and eat traditional food (like it was in Berlin or Kaliningrad in 2017). It became like a lifestyle: to visit Jenny in a new place, to get something new each year.

It is not a simple trip to a concert by our favourite artist. It is more than that. We are learning new places, new cities, new countries, and new lifestyles. To exchange experiences, to give ideas, and to learn something new. We improve ourselves during these journeys. Some like to ski, some like to swim, but we like to visit Jenny's concerts. These meetings are like a classmate reunion in the school every five years.

It has been almost eight years since *My Story* came out, but the song "Here I Am" always plays in my mind when I step outside a plane or a train in a new city: Here I am and I am looking forward to happily spending time in a new place, seeing more sun, and being on a positive wave. Let the shadows from the beginning of the 2010s disappear forever. Let only positive memories stay forever with us. Let the future bring only bright light and faith for a new day. "Now there's nothing that can stop me/All the battles now are won," as Jenny sang in her song "Going Home."

Music from Jenny Berggren makes my life brighter, happier. Her music helped me run away from ordinary days to meet various friendly people and places. Her music helped me come together with people. We are all human, children of nature. We are different and we have our ups and downs, but let us stay together and be ourselves no matter what we face in life.

Thank you, Jenny Berggren—for your music and your active life. With you, my horizon widens.

Meeting Jenny during the International Acer Meeting in Berlin (2013)

ABOUT THE AUTHOR: Aleksandrs Elkins has loved Ace of Base since 1993, obviously, because his first English language cassette was *Happy Nation*. And with it, he fell in love with the band immediately. He has a Master's degree in Mathematics and still makes time for research in the field of fuzzy rough set theory. He works as a mass-valuation expert analyst at the State Land Service of Latvia. His favorite unreleased track from Jenny is "Wait Here."

I Got the Faith that Moves Mountains

by Anja Mummhardt

Jessi and I met in 2002 at a German Acer Meeting in Berlin and became fast friends. In 2004, we travelled together to the International Acer Meeting in Gothenburg, Sweden. During that time, the whole bunch of Acers went to a concert in Hunnebostrand where Jenny performed in a small church. It was the first time we went together to a Jenny concert. Within the last fourteen years, we have been to a lot of concerts. So many that I stopped counting. Most of them in churches. While waiting, we had a lot time to talk about almost everything.

I was never the one who believed in anything like fate, superstition, or God. Sometimes, Jessi had her "wish of the day." I, as a nonbeliever, didn't expect anything to happen. One day, her wish of the day was quality time. I had no idea what that was and asked, "What is quality time?" "Do you never watch Supernanny?" she asked. I just answered, "Ähm, no," so Jessi explained what quality time means. The *Cambridge Dictionary* explains it this way: "Time that you spend with someone, giving them your full attention because you value the relationship." We got quality time with Jenny not only this time, but more often than ever expected. This was the first time I started to see what could happen.

On another day, Jenny wrote something in one of Jessi's books—something she couldn't have known. Both of us still don't know how that was possible, but I can tell you that it changed both of our perspectives. A lot of things happened during the last years, some of them I have no explanation for.

Here are a few examples:

The first example has something to do with my job. It was the second time I went through a time where my job didn't make me happy, rather, it made me sick. So I applied for a new job and sent my CV to different companies. I was quite frustrated because I got no positive response.

Finally, after some weeks, I was invited to an interview. The company was located in an unattractive industrial area. I had the interview with my "future boss," a woman of about forty five. In the very first moment when she opened the door, I knew I would never work in that company, especially with this woman. During the interview, all these old and bad memories from my former boss came back. Not only did she look like my former boss, but she acted in the same way too. My presumptions were later confirmed.

Right after the interview, I was standing on a platform waiting for the next train. I was thinking about my current job and this new position and wondering which option was worse. I decided it was the latter. I had ten days left to quit the job. Otherwise, I would have to wait three more months before I could get out of the contract.

While I sent my CV to different companies, I visited the website of a company I had interviewed with eight months before. Back then, I was the best candidate, but they had to cancel the position due to budget problems. I found this position listed online again, so I sent a short email that I was still interested in the job. Nothing happened. I got no reply, so I decided to upload my CV again. I got a standard confirmation back that they got my mail. Again, nothing happened, so I had given up hope.

The morning after that terrible interview with my "future boss," I told my colleague that we would be working together a little longer. That same evening, I got an invitation for a second interview from the company I had interviewed with eight months before.

Oh my God, I really wanted that job. I wanted it so bad. A friend of mine said, "Send your wish to the universe, but you have to say it out loud." And I thought ironically, "Yeah, sure." It is like Jessi said, "You have to believe and it will happen."

On Monday, I went to the second interview, changed my outfit in the bathroom of my current company, and said out loud, "Please make it happen that I get this job." The interview went well, and on Tuesday, I got positive feedback. On Wednesday, I quit my old job.

And what can I say? Finally, I am very happy with my job.

The second example happened when I came back from London. I was stuck at a tube station because of technical problems. I was standing on the platform hoping that another train was coming that could take me to the airport. But nothing happened, so I asked several people how I could get to the airport, but they had no clue either.

Some of them said they were trying to get a taxi. When I asked if I could join them, they said, "Well, we are already enough people, but we can try." So I went upstairs with them. On the way up, I met a woman from Toronto, Canada, who also had no clue what to do, and I told her that we were trying to get a taxi. So she went with me. The other people were already gone. We lost some time because she couldn't find her card to get out of the tube station. So we lost another five minutes.

Outside the station, it was quite chaotic because everyone was trying to get a taxi. So we asked several people if we could join them, but they all declined. So we asked another Uber driver, but he also said no because we didn't have enough cash. I was running out of time and already thought that I would miss my flight. A moment later, I was sending my wish.

Believe it or not, a few seconds later, a woman was standing right in front of us asking if we wanted go with her to the airport. She had just ordered an Uber taxi. The Canadian woman said we needed fifty minutes to get to the airport. That was exactly the time when my flight was scheduled. Sitting in the taxi, the woman from London checked again and told me that we needed about twenty minutes to get to the airport.

The taxi driver asked which terminal we needed. I had a different terminal than the others, but they had more time. So he asked the other two if it was ok to drop me off first since they had more time. Both of them had no problem. We finally arrived at the airport. I had to get my boarding pass and needed to drop off my baggage. They were quite fast at the counter and the woman at the baggage drop-off printed my boarding pass without asking, which was really cool. I arrived at the gate while the last three people were boarding. I can say I was just in time.

So I was blessed to meet three people: the woman who was so nice to take me to the airport, the taxi driver who arranged to drop me off first, and the woman at the airport.

It doesn't matter how you call it: God, the universe, fate.... Just believe that it can happen and it will. I am still not the person who goes to a church regularly or at Christmas. But meeting people who believe—people like Jenny or my best friend Jessi—was one main reason why I changed my point of view and why I started to believe.

Anja and Jenny in Schwäbisch Gmünd, Germany (2017)

ABOUT THE AUTHOR: Anja lives in Rellingen (a small town near Hamburg) and works as a Human Resources Manager. She is one part of The Jenny Source and co-founder of the former Aceisland website. She worked for websites like 4ever and was the owner of the first Yaki-Da fan page. Anja is a clay artist and designer and runs her own little company. She loves to travel and to take photographs, especially of wildlife. Her favourite songs are "Travel To Romantis," "Numb," and the song "Lär Oss Att Lita På Dig" (from the *Psalmer för Livet* compilations).

Making Life Better

by Frank Carmona

Everything started with Ace of Base, of course. I love them all. When I was a little boy, one of my dreams was to meet them. So last year, when I met Jenny in Chicago, it was so awesome! That was my dream. But I couldn't talk with her easily because the club music was loud. So I want to thank her now: for guiding me with their music and lyrics when I was a little Mexican boy, for allowing me to dream about what I could achieve, and for making my youth better.

My hometown was (and still is) a rough environment. And I never fell into drugs. And gangs never crossed my mind. All because of their music. So I was always listening. Always, all the time.

I've always loved sports as much as music, so the band helped me dream about becoming a professional athlete. A soccer player in this case. Their music helped me stay motivated and confident about my dreams. I was always motivated, but I came up a little bit short...

The band also made my youth better by making my life less tough. I spent my childhood working hard so my family and I could eat at least once a day. I was a little boy working the land with my grandpa, all day, every day back then. It was supposed to be tough for a boy my age, but I didn't feel anything. I was happy and motivated all the time. Everything I did, I did with motivation because their music filled me with confidence. Their music helped me feel strong when I was supposed to be strong and smart when I was supposed to be smart. I was so happy when my grandpa and I finished the day's work because, once at home, Jenny and Linn were waiting for me. I could not wait to get home and listen to Ace of Base.

If the first album were a painting, it would be a priceless Picasso. The harmonics in "All That She Wants," the lyrics and mysterious sound of "Happy Nation," and the Groove Remix of "Don't Turn Around" included on the Mexican release—I just love them! The complete album was great! And the other albums, I love them all too. Their music is unique. Every song has a part that makes me feel good and feel positive.

So, Jenny, I want to thank you for everything you did for me through your music and lyrics. Thank you for making me a better human being.

A freshly signed U2 t-shirt featuring Jenny's autograph (2017)

ABOUT THE AUTHOR: Frank is a fan from Acapulco, Mexico, who now lives in Chicago, Illinois, USA. He is a music lover, sports lover, love lover. He still believes love is the main thing and that we should all add some love into everything we do. He loves every song from the band and from Jenny for different reasons, but his top loves are "Just 'N' Image" and "Give Me The Faith." You can chat with Frank via email at carmonafrancisco324@gmail.com.

Change

by Melinda Visky

We lived in a downtown apartment in simple and modest circumstances when I was little. There was a living room and a kitchen. There was no bathroom toilet in the apartment. The toilet was at the end of the corridor and we bathed in a plastic bathtub. We did not have central heating either. It had to be heated with charcoal. It was a very simple apartment in Budapest.

I was about six years old when my parents divorced. My younger sister was three years old and my younger brother was two years old. Mom was alone with three children. I'm sure it was quite difficult: three children to be educated on their own plus work and the household.

During this time, I was happy. I had nothing else to do except play and enjoy the happiness of childhood. While we played in the yard, Mom always did everything: housework, cooking, washing, and cleaning. But she always kept her eyes on us. How did she do it all herself? I always admired her for that.

During the day, I went to school. Mom would wake us up and get breakfast ready. We would eat breakfast and set off for school. She took my brother and my sister to kindergarten while I walked to school myself since I was big enough to go alone.

After my mom took us to school, she went to work. She worked in an office at a big company in payroll. Mom often brought her work home. When we slept, she worked at night. She slept a few hours, and then she woke us up and got breakfast ready all over again.

Five years later, my mother received an apartment from the local government. This apartment was much more comfortable and spacious. There was a large room, two small rooms, a dining room, a kitchen, a bathroom, a toilet, a pantry, plus central heating—and even a balcony. I remember it was a great joy for my mom to get this apartment.

In August 1989, we moved to the new apartment. Here is where I started a new chapter of my childhood. We were all so excited about the new apartment. The big room was Mom's, the small room was my brother's, and the middle room was for me and my sister.

Some years later, in 1991, a man entered my mom's life. This was the moment when she first met my stepfather and love moved into her life. In 1992, a new family member arrived; my younger sister. I will never forget this moment. She was such a beautiful baby. Even today, I remember everything about the first moment I saw her.

In 1993, a whole new chapter started in my life when I first heard a song by Ace of Base: "The Sign." My enthusiasm started here. I really liked this song. From then on, I watched the music channels whenever I had the chance. I waited for the hit list to see the video again. I enjoyed seeing the band on TV over and over again. And I was really happy when I could see an interview with them.

The more information I got about them, the more I loved them—especially Jenny. For me, she was always my favourite. She is an idol for me. I collected all the posters and articles about them and I wallpapered my room with Ace of Base posters. Mom did not like it at first, but she later accepted that I decorated my room with Ace of Base posters.

One of my classmates made a cassette copy and I have been listening ever since. We had a two-cassette tape player in the dining room. When nobody was at home, I would put the tape in the player and imagine myself standing on stage like Jenny. I grabbed a deodorant bottle or a hairbrush and that was my microphone. I listened to the music and started dancing and pretending that I was a pop star. It is a bit funny now, but back then I enjoyed it.

My mom and I often talked about music. When I heard a new Ace of Base song, I always told her what I thought about it. She also shared the kind of music she liked when she was a teenager. She loved the music of ABBA and Boney M. We had the same musical tastes. For example, ABBA was my second favorite band. She also liked a Hungarian singer, Laslie Komar, whom we called "the Hungarian Elvis Presley." I could list countless performers because we had many of the same musical tastes.

Fifteen years later, in 2008, I was lucky to go to my first and last Ace of Base concert. I did not live at home then. When I told Mom I wanted to go to an Ace of Base concert in Romania, she was happy for me. But she was also afraid because the venue was far away. We kept in contact the whole time I was travelling. When I arrived, I called her. I called after the concert too so she wouldn't worry and know that everything was alright.

The concert was unforgettable. It was a bit strange that there were only three people on the stage, but I enjoyed every moment. Unfortunately, I could not meet the band personally after the concert. But it was so good to share my joy with my mom.

My mother was my best friend in my childhood and later as an adult. We talked a lot about things in life. One day in 2013, my mother called me and told me something was wrong. She found a knot in her chest and she assumed the worst. I tried to be calm, "Don't worry Mom. Everything will be okay," I said. Although, I tell you honestly, in my heart I was so worried but I did not tell her. A couple of months later, she received a date for a mammography. Unfortunately, her concern was not unfounded.

The doctor gave her the bad news: She had breast cancer. Mom was desperate. She did not know what to do. What should we do? How can we go on? We were really worried. We looked for useful solutions and good advice. We searched for useful information on the internet. We talked to some of our friends who were already in a similar situation and we asked for advice on what to do to make sure that my mom was cured.

Eight months later, my mother took several tests. After the tests, a doctor performed surgery to remove one of her breasts. Mom felt like she was not a real woman anymore after that. I told her she had the same value as before her surgery and I told her that she was very important to us. "Don't worry. We will help and support you in everything," I said.

Later, the doctor told my mom she would need chemotherapy. That was a difficult time. I will never forget it. I went with my mom when she started chemotherapy. When we entered the oncology ward, we saw all the people waiting for treatment. Everybody was in a different phase and everybody was struggling to survive. I could see the suffering. It was hard for me to see it without being able to do anything. Mom was upbeat. She spoke with other people who were in a similar situation. And she tried to give strength to others.

Every treatment about was four hours long. My mom was so weak after each one. One time, when we started walking toward the exit after treatment, she grabbed my arm. She was so weak, I was afraid she would collapse. We walked slowly to the exit. It was difficult to walk to the car even.

At home, she stayed in bed because she could not do anything. She had constant nausea, loss of appetite, weakness, and more. Mom's hair began to fall out and then she went bald. When I first saw her hair fall, I tried to pretend I didn't see that this was serious. I'm sure she saw me worrying about it, but I tried to hide it.

Because of all her suffering, she decided to stop chemotherapy and wanted to find healing in a natural cure instead. I was constantly looking for a solution on the internet. I found different capsules, mushrooms, and powders that were specifically recommended for cancer patients. I read good things about these preparations. We started using these formulations along with a different diet. She ate lots of vegetables and followed a guide with different kinds of foods to eat. Because of the preparations and the change in diet, my mother's strength was much better compared to when she had chemotherapy.

Unfortunately, the difficult times were not yet over. March 3, 2014 started like an ordinary workday. My sister called me in the morning and asked me, "Are you sitting or standing?" I did not know what to say. It was strange. "What's wrong?" I asked. She said, "Our brother has passed away." I could not believe what I heard. "Is this real?" "Yes." my sister said, "He felt bad last night, and by the time the ambulance got there, it was too late. The doctors couldn't help."

After gathering myself, I told my boss that I had to leave. When I arrived and saw my brother, I could not understand that this was really happening. It was a shock. When Mom opened the door, she knew something was wrong. We went into the dining room. I asked to her sit down. I did not know how to begin. "How do I tell her this? How do I say this to her gently?"

She just stood there looking at me. She could not understand what I was saying. Then, having realized it, she suddenly collapsed into a chair—with her face buried in her hands—and wept. I cannot even describe this painful feeling of loss. It is the most terrible thing when a mother loses her child. I could not decide what was worse: losing my brother or seeing my mother's pain after hearing such bad news. It was a painful moment that is difficult to describe. I had a hard time losing my brother. I also felt like I had died too.

I focused on school and work. I studied to become a professional cook while working four days a week, twelve to thirteen hours a day. It was tedious to go to school and work so much. I rested one day a week. Of course, besides school and work, I supported my mom too. I tried to visit as much as possible, but visits were usually divided between family who could help.

I usually went to visit Mom on my free day. I stayed there all day and helped with cooking, shopping, cleaning, etc. I also helped before and after school. When I was done, I went home, studied, slept a little, returned, and did it again. It was so tiresome for two years.

In spring 2016, I was working hard and preparing to take my final exam. It was difficult to coordinate both. That's when my mother's condition began to deteriorate. One day, I had to leave work because my mom collapsed in her apartment. I told her she should go to a doctor. She did not want to hear about doctors. I think she was disappointed about losing her son and decided to give up the fight.

It was difficult to watch her get worse. We asked her to visit the doctor, but we knew she would not. She didn't want to do anything. The whole family was upset about her worsening condition. It was stressful and difficult for me—and for the entire family.

One day when I was at work, around April or May, one of my colleagues told me that he heard Jenny was coming to Hungary for a concert. First, I did not hear what he was saying because I was in such a bad mood. Then, when I understood, happiness moved in my heart and the sadness was lost in a moment. Suddenly, I forgot all my problems. I was so very happy in that moment.

When I got home from work, I looked for some information about the event. Fortunately, I found it and called the next day. The organizer gave me the venue name and the concert date: the 25th of June, 2016. He was not able to provide the exact time of the performance but he said he would give me more information later.

While I was waiting on more information from the organizer, I had to struggle with difficult things because my mother's condition was constantly getting worse. There was a lot of stress in the workplace and I was also preparing for my exam. Some weeks later, it was time to take my exam: first was the theory part and then the practical part. When I found out I had passed the exam, I called my mom. She was so proud of me.

A few weeks before the concert, I called the organizer and asked, "Where can I buy tickets for the show?" He said he was not able to organize the concert because he did not get permission. The concert would happen, but he did not know when or where. I was frustrated with the organizer because I did not think Jenny would ever come to Hungary.

On June 5th, I was at home with my mother. She was sleeping, so I let her relax. I returned an hour later and saw that she was drenched in sweat. I bought a cloth to wipe her face. I asked, "How do you feel?" and she answered softly. She was not strong enough to open her eyes. I told my stepfather to help me bring her into the dining room to give her medicine. We brought her in, but we knew something was wrong, so my stepfather called the ambulance.

They tried to stabilize her condition for nearly an hour. The doctor said there was water in her lungs. I heard the doctor say to his colleague, "We must administer morphine." When I heard that, I knew this was trouble. After she was stabilized, they brought her to the hospital in an ambulance.

My stepfather and I got to the hospital before the ambulance. We were worried and nervous. We asked the staff what was happening and they said there was a complication in the ambulance. When Mom was taken out of the car, she was unconscious on a stretcher.

We waited and waited for a word. Finally, a nurse came out from the examination room. She handed me a bag and said there would be no need for it. I asked why and she told me she could not say more. I thought of the worst and became nervous. I opened the bag and found my mom's nightgown and slippers.

I saw the doctors move her from the stretcher to the examination room. We asked the nurse where they were taking her, "She is being transferred to the emergency room because she has to be placed on a breathing machine."

She was put on a breathing machine that first day. Later, the doctors tried to remove it to see if she could breathe on her own. The next day, she was put on it again. The day after that, she was taken off it.

This happened for a week. The doctors decided that Mom needed a tracheotomy to stay on the machine.

After three weeks, the doctors consulted with each other to decide on her future treatment. They said they would move her to the Internal Medicine Department if she improved. One afternoon, her doctor called and told us he was putting her in the Internal Medicine Department. It was a bit strange, being moved so suddenly, but I thought they knew what they were doing since they're the doctors. That Thursday, we went to visit her in the Internal Medicine Department.

The next morning, my sister and her boyfriend went to the hospital to speak with the doctor. After my sister and I spoke on the phone, I had a strange feeling. I felt I had to get away from work to see Mom in the hospital. I arrived at the hospital later that afternoon.

Seeing my mother in her condition was shocking. She was lying in bed with her eyes slightly closed, her head slightly tilted back. She did not respond to us. I moved closer and saw that she was sweating a lot, so we tried to cool her and change the sheets. It was a very hot summer day on the 24th of June, 2016.

She opened her eyes for a moment but her eyes were empty, as if she did not know us. Hours later, at about five o'clock in the afternoon, my stepfather and my sister and her boyfriend returned to the hospital. Mom was still in the same condition as a few hours before.

We were on the balcony getting some fresh air when my other sister told us something was wrong. By the time we got back inside, I saw that my mom's chest was not moving and it frightened me. The doctors arrived after a few minutes and we had to leave the room.

Some minutes later, a doctor came out of the corridor and said he was very sorry but they couldn't do anything more to help my mom. I couldn't call out to my mom. The sensation and consciousness was terrible. When you lose someone who is so close to you, your heart is so sensitive: one moment okay, the other moment hellish.

Since then, I've often thought about the original concert date. It was supposed to take place the day after my mom passed away. As I said, I experienced many emotional waves during this period in my life, times when I felt worse and times when I felt better. After a while, I could not disguise my emotions at my workplace either. I had a moment when I was in an awful mood. My boss told me, "Pull yourself together! Look at Jenny. You know that she has had some difficult moments in her life, but she stood up after the difficult times. And she stands there on the stage making people happy." You know, these words are quite thoughtful because I realized she was right. So I tried to stand up.

The concert organizers set a different date, the 6th of August 2016. I thought I would be okay to attend a concert and this thought gave me strength. I wanted Jenny to see a happy woman enjoying the concert. A happy woman to whom she can give joy because I would finally meet her for the first time after twenty-three years. I thought that if my dream were to come true, then I wanted to be happy when it did! So I had such a double feeling in my heart. I was so excited and so sad sometimes.

And finally, the big day came: August 6th. An hour before the concert, I told my friend Zsuzsi, "Let's go ahead to the stage." As we were few in the first line, we could watch the show from a good spot. We talked to the security guards as we waited for Jenny's concert. I thought, "Okay, this is not bad. Maybe the security guards could help us meet Jenny after the concert."

The concert had a different setup than usual. It had a Hungarian ensemble and two Hungarian vocalists: Rita and David. Before the concert started, the presenter read beautiful and nice words from his phone. Finally, the concert started with the "Intro" from the *My Story* album. The crowd was waiting for Jenny. Everyone shouted loudly. After the "Intro" ended, "Happy Nation" started. The musicians, then the vocalists, and finally Jenny stepped up on the stage. A huge ovation greeted her and the spell started.

When "Happy Nation" was over, Jenny looked happy on stage. We were not many, but she saw that those who were there really loved her. She sang the songs with enthusiasm to a friendly audience. It was nice to see everyone on stage with artists showing respect for her. The Hungarian singers and musicians were also very good. A professional team was on stage together with Jenny.

I remember when "The Sign" was next. It was sung by the audience. It was good to see the joy on her face as we sang together. She looked happy during the whole concert and we were happy too. Especially me, because I could finally see her live in person after twenty-three years.

The next song was "Dying To Stay Alive," and here too, we were singing together with Jenny during the song. Rita said, "It's a big honor to be singing together with Jenny on the stage." And then Jenny said a few words: "For the next song, I need some flowers." Then she went to the side of the stage and returned with a bunch of roses in her hand and gave them to Rita. Rita took the bouquet of roses and said, "Ooh, Jenny, thank you so much. All of them mine?" and laughed. Jenny also laughed, and the audience too.

Then Jenny said: "In this life, we have difficulties. You have, I have. Once, I got a knock on my door. It was a person who told me my father had died that night. And he had taught me that life is a flower and it is so precious in our hands. We only get one life and I believe it won't end. I think I'm going up there, to Heaven, and I will see all of you there. And I will see my father there." When Jenny said these words, I was deeply moved. When she said her dad's there in Heaven, I remembered my mom. That my mom was watching and she was delighted to see me feeling good at the concert. The next moment, I suddenly remembered that she could not be there with me. It was a painful feeling in my heart. I almost cried.

As the concert continued, I was able to shake back into the present moment to enjoy the performance. "Life Is A Flower" was the next song. In this song, there was a part of the chorus where Rita's voice was so beautifully vocal that the sound is still in my mind. It was a beautiful voice. She sang very well together with Jenny.

Then an ABBA song followed. Jenny told us that she had listened to them a lot in her childhood, ever since she was five. The song was: "Gimme! Gimme! Gimme!" followed by "All That She Wants." We sang together with her again. The last song was "Beautiful Life." Everyone started to dance, and Jenny liked that everybody enjoyed the concert. Everybody was having fun.

At the end of the concert, Jenny presented the ensemble and vocalists. Then she went downstairs and left the stage. The audience shouted loudly: "Jenny! Jenny! Jenny! Jenny!" She returned to the stage and sang the slow version of "Don't Turn Around," which she sang beautifully. This song was really touching. I still have goosebumps as I think back to this moment. The whole concert was magical. A beautiful moment it was. She was singing like an angel, and I was glad to be a part of this miracle.

Zsuzsi and I waited after the concert and talked. The presenter said, "Two people at a time to meet with Jenny. Everyone should be patient." I was both patient and excited at the same time. We waited half an hour, or maybe a bit more. I do not know exactly how much time had passed because I was so excited and I was trying to prepare for the meeting. I wanted to make a good impression. I wanted Jenny to know that what she was doing was important to me. And I wanted to tell her that I have a lot of respect and love for her.

When I heard the presenter say "Next!" I got really excited. We went to Jenny. Suddenly, I did not see anyone there. Just her. She asked me something, but I did not hear anything. The place was noisy and I was trying to conceal that I was embarrassed, so I quickly greeted her and introduced myself. She smiled kindly and also greeted us.

Zsuzsi was excited about taking a photo. She started saying that we were going to take a photo. It confused me a bit and I forgot what I wanted to tell Jenny. Jenny noticed the Ace of Base posters in my hand and started signing them, while Zsuzsi handed her phone to a man. He was going to take our pictures together with Jenny. Suddenly, I realized I had to stand next to her to take a picture.

After we were done, I asked Jenny if I could take a picture with just her and me. The picture was snapped and I remembered that I needed to give her my gift. This gift was a package of red pepper spices—a special Hungarian spice mix that is a national treasure. It was packaged with a wooden spoon decorated with the word Budapest. When I gave her the gift, I told her to remember that we really love her. She was surprised and did not expect to get a present. She was very happy and said: "Oh, it's really nice! It's a really nice thing from you." I could see that she was happy.

It was a good feeling for me to stand beside her and express the love that had accumulated in my heart over the past twenty-three years. It was an uplifting feeling and I was ecstatic that my dream had come true. This feeling filled my heart with happiness. It was a miracle. This encounter helped alleviate the pain that I felt after my mom passed away. I'm grateful to Jenny for helping in the difficult moments. I will never forget these wonderful moments.

Then, unfortunately, it was time to say farewell. Everything moved so fast during the meeting. It was hard to realize it was suddenly over. As we walked to the bus stop, I told Zsuzsi, "I do not care when and how, but I'm sure we will attend another Jenny concert again." We talked on the way back and recalled concert moments. We both agreed it was the best concert of our lives and that Jenny is an awesome person.

We really admire her. Her heart is full of love and goodness that is rare in today's world. I think she is an example to many people. She accepts all people no matter their skin color or origin. She loves and respects everyone equally. She knows it is important to believe in the power of love. I think if more people were like Jenny, if it were so, we would live in a much more beautiful and peaceful world.

After the concert, I shared the photos on Facebook, on my own site, and on The Jenny Source. I wanted to share the joy with as many people as possible. After I shared these pictures on Facebook, I met several new acquaintances. One is a woman named Adrienn Döbrössi. Adrienn wrote a message after she saw my pictures on The Jenny Source. She asked to share them in her own fan group too, if I did not mind. (The group is called *Jenny Berggren: The Shining Star*.) I told her, "Of course you can share it and post it to the group." I was curious about the group, so Adrienn and I chatted a lot through Messenger. We had the same opinions about many things connected to Ace of Base and Jenny, so we became friends. Later, I met different people on Facebook like Berta Kovacs and Ilona Major. I did not talk much with Berta and Ilona in the beginning. We were just friends on Facebook. I didn't know them yet.

After the concert and over the next several weeks, I felt very good. I felt good at my workplace and I was able to do more and more work. I was full of energy and felt good in my own skin. I talked a lot about the concert and how good it was to meet Jenny.

The pain that I felt because of the loss of my mother did not go away. I cried a lot when nobody was watching, but I told the outside world that everything was fine with me. I still worked a lot. I felt that "work therapy" helped too and I started to feel a little better.

In August 2017, I met with Berta and Ilona in person. We talked about our Jenny concert experiences and showed each other our concert photos. A couple months later, I heard that Jenny was going to visit Hungary again in November. I immediately shared the good news with Berta and Ilona and we talked online more often.

A few days before the second concert, we started organizing when and where to meet since we wanted to go to this concert together. Meanwhile, Jessi started to organize a meeting for us with Jenny.

After the first concert, I got to know Jessi too. After I shared my photo with The Jenny Source, I started visiting the Facebook page more often. Whenever I saw a post saying I could buy Jenny's t-shirt or book or some item to expand my collection, I wrote a message to Jessi. It was hard to communicate with her because I knew very little English. I used a translation program to make communication more simple. Sometimes I can write stupid things, but fortunately we always understood each other.

I'm glad to know Jessi and I think she is so kind and I'm very thankful. So I think Jessi is a very important person in my life. Or, I will say on behalf of other fans, she is so important to everyone. Without her work, we would have much less information about Jenny, much less chance of meeting with Jenny, and much less chance of my dream coming true. So I can say in the name of all the fans that we love and respect Jessi very much. Without her, we would not have as many miracles in our lives. I'm grateful for her, because without her help, I would not have met Jenny a second time. Without her, I could not have experienced these wonderful moments.

The second concert (25th of November 2017) was a bit short: only four songs. Jenny sang four of the best-known Ace of Base songs: "Happy Nation," "Don't Turn Around," "The Sign," and "Beautiful Life." We enjoyed the concert and Jenny's performance. The atmosphere of the concert was so magical. She seemed to be very happy on the stage. As she moved closer to the crowd, I saw her looking for us there in the crowd, and her dancers were looking for us too.

You know, it's great to see her on stage. She gives a fantastic show. You get lots of love from her, and when you feel this love, all your problems are eliminated at once. You arrive into a completely different world where love prevails and it fills your heart with gladness. From this fantastic feeling, you want to be yourself more and more, so that when you return to reality, you will have something to give you strength.

After the concert, we found the meeting place quickly. It was so good to know that we would meet Jenny soon. I felt that she was looking forward to the meeting. We stood near the corridor and waited for Jenny's security man to arrive. While we waited, we talked. The show continued on stage, but I could not pay attention because I was so excited waiting to meet Jenny.

When I saw her, I felt such a happiness, I cannot describe it. I just looked at her and thought, "Is she really here? I cannot believe this." She said we should move closer, so we did. Jenny wanted to go to a quieter place to get a better conversation because the place was so loud. She asked the bodyguard, but he said there was no opportunity to move.

From the first moment, Jenny was so nice with everyone. She was delighted to meet with us and everyone was so happy. It was fantastic. She greeted us very kindly, shook hands with everyone, and gave a kiss to everyone like we were old friends. It was a wonderful feeling that she was so kind to us.

She suddenly turned to me and asked me how I was. I was so surprised that I answered in Hungarian. This was a bit funny. I was embarrassed because I first spoke in Hungarian, but I quickly answered in English. I told her I was excited to meet her again, that we met at another event last year. I also told her that I did not know English well. She smiled kindly and waved with her hand that it did not matter. I showed her the photo and she signed it for me. Jenny met with Zsuzsi and then she continued down the line to meet everybody else.

In the next moment, I noticed that people started taking photos with Jenny. Everyone wanted to take a photo at the same time with her. Jenny was also surprised that everybody took photos at the same time. But then she finally faced the camera that was in front of her.

I watched the events from the background and waited for the right moment to give her a second gift. This gift was a fridge magnet with a Budapest label, a small mug with a Hungary label, and a little angel. I put it all in a small gift box labeled Merry Christmas. It's true that Christmas was a month later, but I knew that this was my only chance, so it was a good time to express my admiration for Jenny. I chose this gift because I wanted to give a gift related to Hungary so she would remember how much Hungarian fans love her.

I waited for everyone to finish taking pictures. When it was over, I went to Jenny with the gift in my hand. And for a few seconds, I just stood there. She looked at me, smiled kindly, and waited for me to say something. I was waiting to say something too, but I couldn't say anything. Suddenly, I was blocked. I couldn't speak. It was quite embarrassing. I don't remember exactly when I gave her the gift because my head was empty for a few seconds. I could not find the words. Then suddenly, I remembered a sentence: "I'm so thankful!"

When I spoke this sentence, I felt in my heart that all of my love and respect was here in these words. I looked at Jenny and saw that she was moved by this moment, and it touched me. I saw her tears and I could not continue my sentence. We just looked at each other for a few seconds. We were both moved and could not speak. Jenny looked at me and smiled kindly. Then she took hold of my hand and I got two kisses from her to my face. It was great to see that she was made happy from my kind gesture.

Then we took a photo together. I stood next to her. She moved close to me and I hugged her and she put her head on my head. It was a good feeling to feel the pure and sincere love from her. Some of the others who had not taken a photo with Jenny went to take one. Jenny was so nice to everyone.

I am so happy to be part of the miracle that surrounds Jenny. I admire her so much because when she sings, she reveals her feelings on stage and it is fantastic to see.

I don't just admire her for her work on stage. Her heart is full of love and anywhere she goes in the world, she gives a piece of love to all people. She is able to make this ugly world more beautiful.

I don't know if you have had the chance to experience the miracle of meeting Jenny. If not, I hope it will happen one day because everybody needs such wonderful moments in this noisy world. Both concerts were an unforgettable experience for me. I'm grateful to the Lord for giving me these wonderful moments in Jenny's world.

During my life, I have seen the sunny and the shaded side of life. There were tribulations that were difficult. There were situations where I thought I could not overcome the obstacles, but I always stood up and took the fight and I never gave up. My mom taught me to fight and to believe and to trust. She also showed me the power of love. Jenny too showed me the power of love. They both showed me how the power of love can change a life—and the world.

Moments after Jenny received an early Christmas gift from Melinda (2017)

ABOUT THE AUTHOR: Melinda lives in Budapest, the capital of Hungary. She loves nature, good food, good company, animals, and good music. She hates lies and injustice. In her relationships, the most important traits are honesty, respect, and love because she herself is a kind person who tries to find the common good in everyone. Her favorite band is Ace of Base and her favorite singer is Jenny Berggren. You can contact Melinda at: facebook.com/melinda.visky

Ace of Base in My Life

by Raphael Ferreira dos Santos

It was one of the most important days of my life. My friends and I were watching TV one Sunday in 1994 and the show was going to host the band Ace of Base. Their songs, their sounds are unmistakable. At that moment, listening to Linn and Jenny, my world stopped. I knew that my life would never be the same.

It started a new love, a race to collect photos, songs, vinyls, cassette tapes—everything that belonged to the band. Everything to form my collection (my private treasure). Everything I did in my everyday was related to my favorite band: from clothes, hair, beard, and even poses for photos—all the same. I just thought of being them. It was the same for my cousin Lidiane, who also loves Jenny forever.

In the city of São Paulo in 2011, I got to know the band's second lineup. Seeing Jonas and Ulf, I was sure that one day I could meet Jenny too. After years, came the confirmation that I could meet my queen, my inspiration: Jenny.

I traveled to Lima, Peru in January 2017 to attend the biggest show of my life. My friends, Acers, and I got to meet our queen. My God! So much love, friendship, and respect she showed for her fans.

During the show, she wore a necklace I gave her. I wore a t-shirt and held a banner during the show, both with photos of Jenny. When she waved to me from the stage, my heart stopped. Such a huge emotion. Unmistakable, eternal, our singer Jenny!

I thank God for experiencing these unique and magical moments alongside those I love so much.

Jenny, you are my world! Thanks for everything!

Raphael with his "Here I Am" banner in Lima, Peru (2017)

ABOUT THE AUTHOR: Raphael is a fan from Rio Novo, Minas Gerais in Brazil. He is a math teacher who loves his profession and his students. He is the father of two boys, Matheus and João Marcelo. Raphael enjoys reading books, but his biggest passion is music. His favorite songs have always been "The Sign" and "Donnie" and the voices of Jenny and Linn have always been some of his greatest inspirations. He cannot help but listen to them. Forever Ace of Base!

Follow That Dream

by April Robertson

"Some people come into our lives and touch our heart so deeply that we will never be the same again." – Unknown

My life has never been the same since Ace of Base entered my life. It was the fall of 1993. A family friend who was visiting Baton Rouge, Louisiana, played a mixtape for us. On it was "All That She Wants." The mystical sound of the flute, short burst of the sax, and seductive vocals drew me in.

In the beginning of 1994, I was in my room listening to the radio while doing my homework. The DJ announced that Ace of Base had a new single titled "The Sign." I couldn't help but sit there and stare at the radio as it played. Homework at that moment became the last thing on my mind.

"The Sign" sealed the deal for me. I begged my mother to buy the album for me as a birthday present. In mid-March of 1994, she drove me to the mall so I could show her what the album looked like. When we got home, I ran into my room, grabbed my portable CD player, and played the album over and over. I even made a cassette copy to play on my stereo. I drove my parents and brother crazy! My dad said the constant drumming made him think of island natives being restless. I would roll my eyes every time he said that.

Most of the students at my school listened to grunge, hip-hop, R&B, and country. If there were any other Ace of Base fans in my midst, I didn't know it. There were times I heard people make snarky remarks about the band. I wanted to tell them they were missing out on some good music. It was better than most of the Top 40 on the radio.

For the longest time, I had thought that the band was from the United States. Before the age of searching the internet, I had to rely on MTV or VH1 for information about Ace of Base. One day, I heard a VJ on MTV referring to them as "Swedish Meatballs," and another time, on VH1 as "the new ABBA." Me, being a researcher at heart, began to find any information I could about this Scandinavian country that had introduced the world to SAAB, Volvo, dynamite, and the three-point safety belt. I went to my brother's room and found a vintage set of encyclopedias my parents owned. I grabbed the copy marked S-T, and turned to the topic that mattered most to me: Sweden. It may have been seventeen year-old information, but it was all I had.

More specifically, I wanted to know where exactly in Sweden Ace of Base was from. I found out after I read an article in a teen magazine. Back to my source from 1977 to find out about Göteborg. I wanted to get a sense of the cultural differences between Swedes and Americans. Sure, the library probably had more updated information, but it wasn't within walking distance, and I didn't want my mother asking one hundred questions on why I was researching Sweden.

Around this time, I sent a letter to a travel agency asking for information about Sweden. A few weeks later, I received a huge wall map and magazine. I smiled every time I looked at it because I felt like I had a link to the band.

Around the beginning of 1995, I heard that Ace of Base's second album was due to be released in the US in October. I remember being so happy that I started jumping up and down in my room with excitement. However, I didn't realize I had a monster growing inside of me—depression. No matter how many times I listened to *The Sign*, it didn't keep the depression at bay.

On October 27th, while walking home from school, I revealed to a friend about the sexual abuse I endured as a child. From the age of about three until I was eight or nine, a neighbor my parents trusted sexually molested me. When I got the courage to tell my parents, they believed me but didn't pursue charges. Sexual abuse tests didn't exist back then, so it would have been my word against the man.

This so-called friend told me I should have killed myself to get out of this crazy world after I told her I had contemplated suicide. Her comment allowed the growing monster to mutate into a hellish nightmare. That night, I wrote a suicide note, swallowed a handful of pills, and laid in my bed praying to die. It must have been a few hours later when I felt someone slapping my face. My brother and his girlfriend had come in from a date and found me.

I was taken to a psychiatric facility and admitted into the youth wing. My mother tried to convince me to go back home. I looked her directly in the eyes and told her I would find some way to end my life no matter what. I just wanted the pain to end. One thing that stopped me was realizing I wouldn't be able to pursue my dreams if I was buried six-feet underground.

In the early morning hours of the 28th, I lay in my hospital bed listening to the rain outside. I started crying and asked God to help me. It was at that time I felt Him closer than I ever had before.

On the 30th, my 72-hour stay in the hospital was over. The first thing I wanted to do was go to the record store and buy Ace of Base's album. After we met with my psychologist, my dad drove me to the now-defunct Blockbuster Music store. The album release date had been pushed back, but the first single was available.

That night, while driving on the freeway back home, I heard the opening chords of "Beautiful Life" blast through my headphones. A rush of euphoria shot through my body. Ace of Base was back with more feel-good music!

The band's music took me to a better reality than what I was living at that time. Whenever I had a bad day at school, all I had to do was put on some Ace of Base and my worries melted away. Sometimes, I would imagine I was in a disco dancing the night away to their music and just letting go of my troubles.

On the 14th of November, Dad drove me back to Blockbuster Music so I could buy the new album, *The Bridge*. One of the features I liked about the booklet was the set of backstories behind the songs. It helped the listener understand the meaning behind the lyrics.

When the CD got to track six, it was as if time had stopped. Listening to "Ravine" was almost like listening to my feelings the night I attempted suicide. An overwhelming wave of emotions came crashing over me. I didn't know how to cope with it. I just stuffed it down inside, like I always did.

The next time I listened to the song, anger erupted inside of me like a volcano. I remember I got so mad that I punched my closet door hard and broke a wooden slat in it. (I had a louver door back then. My mother said I was lucky I didn't break my hand.) That same day, I sat down and wrote my first set of lyrics.

Writing allowed me to get out emotions that I had a hard time expressing externally. Inspiration for lyrics can strike at different times. Sometimes, all it takes is reading something in the newspaper, listening to a conversation between others, or hearing a word or emotion in a song. Inspiration is all around us every day.

Ace of Base influenced me to get back into learning how to play music and experiment with lyrics. I began to teach myself how to play the guitar with the student books my brother used when he took lessons. Later, I learned that playing by tabs rather than chords was easier to learn. I also began playing the piano again. I experimented with chords and tried to match what I heard in the band's music.

The same year *The Bridge* was released, I was in Girls' Show Choir in school. I had played the clarinet in the school band in sixth and seventh grade. By grade eight, I wanted to sing more than anything, so I tried out for choir. Singing along to AoB, I believe, helped me make it into choir. Listening to Malin and Jenny helped me develop my voice and style.

At the beginning of the school year, we were told we would have to do a group or solo performance as a final grade. When the choir director asked what I was going to do, I told her I was singing solo. When she asked what song, I replied, "'Experience Pearls' by Jenny from Ace of Base." The groans that shot across the room were of disapproval. However, they were surprised to hear this beautiful ballad. The choir director said I did a great job. I am quite an introverted person, so when I sang, most of my classmates were surprised to hear how well I sang.

"Experience Pearls" inspired me to write what I would consider a b-side. The lyrics tell the story of a person who has passed unexpectedly, and they watch over their significant other on Earth. They tell them they will always be here when they speak their name. The name of it is "I'll Always Be Here." In 1998-99, a fellow Acer named Amelia composed music for it. It was going to be recorded for a project that never got off the ground. One day, my tape player decided it was hungry and ate the tape with the music. I have re-worked the lyrics since then but I haven't tried to get the music re-done. One day, I will though. When that day comes, it will still be a ballad but recorded in the style of symphonic metal. Maybe I will try to submit it to a publishing company or just keep it in my personal files.

I have continued to write lyrics over the years. I have them in a folder tucked away in a safe place. In 2011, a well-known member of the Ace of Base community named Claes tried to get some of my lyrics published. Unfortunately, the publishing group wasn't interested in what I had written. But at least I had Claes, someone who believed in me being a good lyricist and who had worked side by side with the band and Jenny for many years.

Currently, I am taking a break from writing lyrics to focus on writing a book that has been in the works since 1994. The story was inspired by Ace of Base and the main character by Jenny. I'm putting my many years of research into Sweden and Göteborg to good use by having the story take place there. A few years ago, someone tried to convince me to change the setting to the United States. I told them it's staying where it is because it's been that way for twenty-something years. My plan is to self-publish it in digital and paper format soon.

Jenny inspired me to keep following my dreams. I don't know how, but I know my words will make an impact on the world. Keep fighting for what you believe in and want, even if you think you are standing alone. There is a team of thousands behind you that you can't see. Thank you, Jenny. Because of you and faith, I never gave up.

April having lunch with friends

ABOUT THE AUTHOR: April lives in Baton Rouge, Louisiana, USA and is currently training to be a dog groomer. She enjoys making pendants and dog collar charms out of polymer clay. She also loves to read, meditate, study ancient spiritual texts, and listen to different types of music (mainly symphonic metal). She still listens to Jenny's music when the mood strikes. You can follow her on Instagram at: aprilrains81.

Acer Animal Cop

by Annje Hultgren

To say that Ace of Base and Jenny Berggren have had a positive influence and impact on my life would be a tremendous understatement. Jenny and Ace of Base came into my life during my influential teenage years. They helped set the tone for the decisions I would make and for the direction that my life would take.

I was born to immigrant parents: a German mother and Swedish father. Although I was raised primarily in the United States, I have strong ties to my Swedish and German heritage. So when Ace of Base emerged onto the music scene, I became a fan before the vast majority of anyone in the States knew of their existence. I was immensely proud of my Swedish heritage when they came onto the scene. In much the same way, I imagine, that Swedes were when ABBA came around during their time.

Ace of Base quickly developed a phenomenal fanbase of tight-knit fans and we referred to ourselves as "Acers." I became fast friends with many other Acers from all over the world and developed lasting friendships with them. I remain in close contact with them to this day through email, social media, text messaging, phone calls, and even snail mail and visits to each other.

One of these Acer friendships turned out to be more than I could have imagined. As a young teenager, I befriended an Acer boy in North Germany and we remained in contact throughout the years. I never would have imagined him reciprocating any romantic feelings towards me. But, alas, I was wrong. After several failed attempts at meeting him due to my painful shyness and convincing myself there was absolutely no way he would have any interest in me, the day came when I booked a flight to North Germany. (Before that, I always traveled to Germany to visit my family in the Nürnberg area.) This flight would start in Phoenix, then to Los Angeles, then to Chicago, then to Frankfurt, and finally, Hannover.

During the flight, I tried not to psych myself out and I gave myself (not so successful) "pep talks." He and I had a lot in common and we seemed to have chemistry. Even my Acer cousin Anja told me he would never have been so adamant to invite me all the way over to North Germany to spend time with him if he wasn't interested. She further reminded me that Germans are brutally honest people and don't say things they don't mean.

I was still not very good at calming myself down during the flight. The butterflies in my stomach made me feel like I was going to explode. That's when the calming effects of "Travel to Romantis" came blasting through my headphones. It certainly seemed fitting—I was travelling to North Germany to finally meet the sweet (and very handsome!) shy German boy who I had long ago befriended and developed feelings for. So, in a sense, I was traveling "to Romantis." And suddenly, my breathing was calm and I no longer had heart palpitations. I could focus on the rest of the flight, enjoy my time off from work, and look forward to making new memories in one of my favourite places: Germany, a.k.a my other home.

I exited the plane and walked down the stairs to the waiting area. There was my beloved Stefan staring up at me with his beautiful grey eyes. The way he was smiling when he saw me made my heart melt! He gave me a huge hug and it eased any worries that I had. Early in the evening, we sat and talked. He poured his heart out to me about his feelings, which of course, I reciprocated.

We discussed the challenges of an international relationship and agreed that the challenges would only be temporary. We decided we were willing to compromise on location: we would work together to decide where we would live. And that sealed our fate. We knew then that we were a perfect match, destined to be together. We began to embark on an emotional journey of an international relationship.

Eights months later, I was back in Germany for my birthday, Christmas, and New Year's. Little did I know that my shy German prince had something planned. At midnight on my birthday, he woke me up, got down not on one knee but two, held out a ring—and asked me to marry him! This definitely fit the "Travel to Romantis" lyrics!

We discussed where to live and I told him I had given a lot of thought to the pros and cons of places we could live together. He was certain he wanted us to live in the US. And I would compromise and agree to it, as long as he knew we had to return to Germany at least once a year for my sanity. We then began the long, complicated, and frustrating steps of navigating the current US immigration system. But he was worth it, and now I am happily married to my German prince.

And I can thank our mutual interest in Ace of Base and Jenny for that. Because, without those factors, he and I would never have crossed paths and I would likely be still single to this day. Jenny probably never knew she was also a cupid and inadvertent matchmaker in disguise!

So thanks to Ace of Base and Jenny for changing my destiny so I would not become a single spinster with 300 cats—instead, we have nine cats of our own. We also take on medical foster cats and kittens on a regular basis to help them find their forever homes.

It was during the release of *The Bridge* that Ace of Base and Jenny had a fundamental impact on my career path. Since I was a young child, I have always been compassionate towards animals and involved in animal welfare. My German *Oma* instilled this in me. We always rescued cats, dogs, and wildlife, and raised various foster cats and kittens when I was young. I volunteered at local animal shelters in Pennsylvania and Toronto, but animal welfare concerns were always bothersome to me, so I longed to be more involved on a larger scale.

The songs "Perfect World" and, of course, Jenny's "Ravine" were instrumental in pushing me further to be more involved, to pursue my heart's desire—to be a Humane Officer. Listening to the depth of the lyrics in "Ravine" hit home with me. Even though I am but one small person, standing in a deep, dense "Ravine" (a.k.a the world), I can decide to make a difference and impact in the world, no matter how small. It can cause a ripple effect for the greater good. The songs helped me take my intentions to another level. I decided I was going to achieve my career goal, and I dove into it full force.

I began at the bottom and worked my way up. I started working in an animal shelter taking care of administrative duties, animal intakes, and licensing. And soon, I was recruited to take on community outreach tasks by educating the public on the feral cat situation. I started working weekends in the shelter clinic, helping with spay and neuter surgeries, giving medical treatments to sick animals, and working side by side with the shelter veterinarian.

One of the Lieutenants was working with a shelter veterinarian on an animal cruelty case and I was assisting. The Lieutenant saw I had a talent for animal forensics, so I was invited to apply to become a full-fledged Humane Officer and Animal Cruelty Investigator. I applied and was accepted for the position.

And true to Jenny's style, never satisfied with being complacent, I wanted more. I wanted to make the most of my position—to become an even greater asset to the animals I was sworn to advocate for and protect. I took all the formal training I could find and gained certification in many areas of animal welfare. I also became a certified EAMT (Emergency Animal Medical Technician) and Veterinary Technician. I wanted to be able to triage and administer lifesaving care in the event of an emergency.

One such example involved my own cat, Giselle, a two-year-old blue cream tabby Domestic Shorthair. I was on call when a 911-emergency report came through. The caller was frantic, reporting that he found a cat that he thought had rabies. I asked for more information. He said he owned a construction company that was about to break ground on a new master-planned community in the middle of nowhere. There were no homes or businesses in any direction for miles. He owned a portable construction trailer created for business purposes. And on that late Sunday afternoon in July, he took a trip to the work trailer to prepare paperwork. That's when he heard a faint cry and found Giselle underneath the trailer in horrible condition. She was laying on her side, unable to move or stand, gasping for air, and foaming at the mouth.

I immediately suspected heat stroke, as it gets extraordinarily hot in the summer (upwards of 130°F/54°C). While I was en route, the man decided to consult "Dr. Google." He looked up heat stroke and took it upon himself to carry out treatment. He placed the cat in a plastic container filled with water and ice. By the time I arrived, this cat had suffered from both hypothermia and hyperthermia in a span of five minutes. She was in critical shape, so I immediately started to warm her up slowly and massage her to keep her alert. I took her to the nearest emergency veterinary clinic and requested a full neurological blood screening, since heat stroke is a neurological condition. Everything was done to stabilize her and she was given a guarded prognosis. I took it upon myself to foster her and get her through this.

After about two months of physical therapy and force feeding her, she started to walk and eat on her own again. She still has some slight neurological deficits due to the brain damage, but it is minor and difficult to notice unless you have a veterinary medical background. Due to what I went through with her, I ended up adopting her myself. She is now a happy and healthy spoiled house cat. Giselle is just one of the many rescues I have helped save through my training and background knowledge.

When Hurricane Katrina hit, there were thousands of animals in need of rescue. I was recruited by the Humane Society of the United States as part of a task force team. We traveled to the disaster zone to rescue animals in need, catalogue them, and reunite them with their families.

Arizona, the state I live in, has a brutal summer season. Annual wildfires place not only cats and dogs in grave danger, but horses and other livestock and wildlife as well. Due to my experience with Hurricane Katrina, I have been recruited each summer to assist with rescue and transport during the wildfire outbreaks. My house almost always has at least one foster cat or kitten, usually a medical case requiring specific medical and rehabilitation care.

Most recently, I have taken inspiration from Jenny's Voi involvement. Like her, I want to help where I can with the talent and skills I have. I want to help animals that have no voice and do my small part to enable them to have better lives, removing them from cruel or neglectful situations and getting them the medical care they need.

I am eternally grateful towards Jenny and Ace of Base for doing what they do. They have helped mold my young mind into the person I am today and they have brought together such an amazing group of Acers who have built such a compassionate community. I am happily married to one of them—an amazing German Acer who I get to share my life with.

Jenny still continues to have a positive influence and impact on the worldwide community. And, although she may not fully realize it, she continues to be an outstanding role model and continues to make me proud to be Swedish.

Annje taking care of one of her many rescue animals

ABOUT THE AUTHOR: Annje was born in Toronto, Canada, and raised in Pennsylvania, United States, to a father from Sweden and a mother from Germany. Her home is host to an ongoing parade of foster animals recuperating from injury until they can be adopted. In her free time, she enjoys travelling, hiking, exploring, and mountain biking together with her husband from Germany.

An Ode to Jenny

by Rinat Meshulam

Dear Jenny,

How can I describe in words how much your lyrics of your solo career and the lyrics of Ace of Base have affected my life since you became famous in 1992? No word in the world can describe my admiration for you and the rest of the band. I especially admire you Jenny, and Malin too, because both of you have wonderful singing talent. And because of the special voices that both of you have: voices of angels, voices that reach deep into my being, tug at the strings of my heart, and cause me to feel optimistic in moments of sadness.

Your music provides huge happiness during exciting moments and reminds me that it is possible to overcome every obstacle in life during times of sadness. I am happy when I listen to the lyrics you sing and the music played by Jonas and Ulf. Thank you for the music, the texts, and the power that you give me. Your music is always there for me.

I've never seen how you look because I'm blind from birth, but I fell in love with your voices. I can tell what special people you are, so I do not need to imagine how you look. I especially enjoy the fun and joyous feeling I get from listening to your voices. I admire that you have taken the talent God has given you and used it as a blessing for your fans. Your music and lyrics are more than precious.

Jenny, I always wanted to tell you how much you mean to me as a person and how much I appreciate your talent in singing and writing, even though I do not know you personally. I identified a lot with the lyrics that you sang in Ace of Base and, of course, when you started your own solo work. You are an inspiration to me in writing my own poems and songs.

Ever since I first heard "All That She Wants," the song that was played on every radio station in Israel without interruption in 1992, I connected with the lyrics of your songs—and your unique music—and I started to admire Ace of Base.

When I was a girl, I wanted to understand the meaning of the words you sang and your songs motivated me to start learning a new language, English, which later opened a door to the world. And so I was able to establish contacts and friendships for life with people from different countries around the world. The first song I wanted to understand was "Wheel of Fortune" because it was, and still is, one of my favourite songs from your first album, *Happy Nation*. I always love to listen to it and sing along with you.

Since 1992, whenever I hear Ace of Base songs on the TV or on the radio, I turn up the volume and sing together with the lyrics and texts that have become a part of me. I can't divide them from my life. One of the songs I've always liked to hear, and one that has influenced me, is "Beautiful Life." The most encouraging part of the song I like to hear is: "Take a walk in the park when you feel down. There's so many things there that's gonna lift you up. See the nature in bloom, a laughing child. Such a dream."

Another song and another situation that had a great impact on me was when I heard Jonas and Ulf give an interview on an Israeli radio station in 1995. They said that you wrote a song called "Ravine" and it tells the story of a person who broke into your parents' house and tried to attack you with a knife. I remember that I took very hard what they said. And after listening to your song, I cried for a long time. A few days later, I wrote a poem in Hebrew called "The Wound That Was Never Healed," which tells from my point of view what you described in your song "Ravine." Of course, I was glad you survived and it always encouraged me to hear the words that God has always been there by your side, despite the nightmare. You never lost faith, as expressed in the song: "I'll tell you, I'll tell you what, He was the only one there. I am standing here in my Ravine. Once again, I see a piece of the sky and my joy'll never be denied 'cause I was meant to be here. The only place on earth where you are near."

Another unforgettable moment in my life was when you released your third album in 1998. I fulfilled a dream on the 24th of September when the four members of Ace of Base appeared on *MTV Select.* I called in and was able to talk to you about the *Flowers* album. The excitement of hearing your voices over the phone caused me to forget my English for a second. The conversation with you was exciting for me—and the euphoria I felt after affected me for days.

I got two CDs from you, the "Cruel Summer" single and *Flowers,* which were both signed. The show's producer wanted to call me a week later to tell me my prizes were being sent. Because of Yom Kippur, a holy day in Israel, my phone was closed, so she could only hear my answering machine with the background sounds of "Cruel Summer."

When *My Story* was released in 2010, I remember waiting and getting excited as I waited for the disc to arrive in the mail. Since I could not get it in stores in Israel, I ordered it from an internet store in Sweden. The songs played on my CD player and also in my mind. Two songs I identified with strongly at that time were "Gotta Go" and

"Going Home." "Gotta Go" strengthened me when I decided to move on and overcome unrequited love. And "Going Home" surrounds me with the feeling of family and home.

There are many more moments connected to Ace of Base and Jenny in my life, but I have to write one more. One moment is unforgettable for me—a moment I never believed would ever come true in my life. This moment happened when you appeared in 2017 in Oberhausen. For the first time, I could hear you live and meet you face to face. I cannot describe in words the tremendous excitement I felt when you shook my hand and when you talked to me. Every time I think back on this moment, my heartbeat accelerates and I remember every detail of the fan meeting with you. That day I met you fulfilled my big dream.

I want to thank you for the joy and the encouragement you give to all your fans. Thank you, dear Jenny, and I love you for what and who you are. Thank you for your wonderful music and lyrics. You are an inspiration to me.

And now, after I met you, I want to thank you for your joy and the calm you give to fans all over the world. Thank you for your wonderful music and lyrics. I wish you all the best in your world.

Israel's number one fan,
Rinat Meshulam

Rinat fulfilling a big dream in Oberhausen (2017)

ABOUT THE AUTHOR: Rinat was born in Israel and has grown up in a city called Bat Yam. She is full of humour and loves to use her special sense of humour often. Singing is part of her life, and not just in the shower. She loves to listen to lots of different kinds of music, but especially children's songs. She is a teacher and finds a lot of satisfaction in her work educating children. Writing poems is an important hobby for her, and she hopes that one day somebody will publish those poems. She looks forward to getting in touch with other fans from all over the world: rinatush1@gmail.com.

Live for Today

by Ilona Major

I was born in Hungary in a small town called Oroszlány. I love music, travel, tennis, hiking, basketball, and bicycling. I also love nature, silence, and tranquility. My friends are good-natured, cheerful, patient, and good-hearted. I have been disappointed with friends, and with love too. But I got back up and found ways to enjoy life because it is important to live for today.

I was fifteen when I first heard "All That She Wants." I bought the first cassette and I listened to it with Endre, a cousin I grew up with, and we decided that this was our music. Later, I played it for my friends and they loved it too. When we got together, we always imitated the videos and we sang. We dressed up and used a can of hairspray as a microphone. We were four people, so it was not difficult to divide the roles.

I collected posters, pictures, articles, badges, CDs. Everything that was related to Ace of Base. We listened to Ace of Base and loved it. It made me feel more alive. We talked a lot about going to a concert and visiting Sweden one day, but it was not possible then because we were too young.

In October 2012, I finally got to go to Sweden and Gothenburg with Endre. We had decided in our childhood that we would visit when we were older—and so it was. When we reached Gothenburg, I was crying out of happiness! I was astonished. I was so happy and I could not believe I was there.

Endre and I tried to walk around the whole city, but we could not see everything within six days. I would have liked to visit the amusement park Liseberg, but unfortunately, it was closed. So we started exploring the city instead. We went to the Opera House and walked around it and it was beautiful. We followed the harbour, which was packed with boats, and it was more beautiful still. We arrived at an office building called Skanskaskrapan. We went to the top using an elevator then looked down at the city from the window. It was wonderful!

We came and went, roaming and taking pictures of our adventures. We even had a *fika*. This is where people sit, have coffee, and talk while eating pastries. Endre had the famous Swedish cinnamon bun and I had a slice of carrot cake. I found my shop because there is a grocery store there called "ICA." This is my nickname in Hungary. I was so happy to see it and it was so funny.

On day three, we went to Slottskogen park. We saw a lot of churches on the way. There were small houses with grass on the roofs and a little lake in the park. A peacock walked up to us there. He wanted food at all costs and went to everybody asking. He was gentle and had a beautiful plumage. It was blue and his body was green, yellow, brown, white, and gold. The horses were impressive too. We also saw deer, penguins, and all kinds of animals. We went to Skansen Kronan after that, which is a fortress on a hill. Our next stop was the Botanical Gardens with a variety of different flowers and plants.

In the morning, we had breakfast and went out to explore the city some more. We went to the Universeum Science Centre. They had robots, a shredder, simulators, ocean fish, etc. It was a fun place. We also went to an island named Vrångö, which was cosy. Unfortunately, the last day of our trip had arrived. The city and its people were very nice. I loved it!! I was sure I would come back again.

In 2016, I learned that Jenny would play a show in Hungary. It was my dream come true. I remember I was excited for the concert on August 6th. I went with my friend, her son, and my daughter. When Jenny arrived on stage, I realised that she was actually in my country. I did not believe it, seeing her there in front of me.

My mother, who had passed away when I was younger, came to my mind during "Don't Turn Around" and I sensed it. It was like she was there with us. My daughter and my friend's son danced during "Beautiful Life." I was proud that my little girl saw Jenny live. Jenny sang both her own songs and ABBA, which I love very much. The concert was just a bit short, but I really enjoyed it. Fantastic!

Later, we had the chance to meet Jenny in person. We went straight to the queue. I was so excited! We were waiting for her and I was almost in the middle of the crowd. Jenny's book *Vinna Hela Världen* was in my hands. When she saw it, she was happy and we were greeted in Swedish.

I planned everything beforehand, including what I was going to say. Of course, nothing came out of my mouth when it was time. I had so much to say, but I was so excited, I forgot what my name was. My friend helped me out. She reminded me to say my name so I could speak. Jenny could tell that I was so excited. She spoke with me and took my hand, greeting me like a good friend. We took a photo, but it did not turn out so well, so we asked a security guard to let us go back to the end of the line. He let us return and take a good picture.

Afterwards, we said we did not believe it. We had waited twenty-four years and our dream came true! It was worth the wait! Jenny was a very nice, sweet person. An angel!!

Halfway home, I was sitting in the car staring out the window. I still could not believe it. "Dream or Reality?" I had so much happiness in my heart that I had met my big favourite!

In May 2017, I was lucky enough to go back to Sweden. I went to Stockholm and Uppsala for a super weekend. I tried to see everything during those two days. I arrived and waited for my friend. She and I went to the hotel and checked in. We wanted to explore Stockholm, but unfortunately it was late in the evening by then.

We went out the next morning to explore the town. It was a great place to go and it was great to see the underground stations because of all the exciting and colorful and unusual decorations. It was a nice place to experience. It turned out that the "Living in Danger" video was shot here too, which was great to learn about and see.

After that, we continued on our journey to the Vasa Museum. The museum houses a beautiful big ship that is 69m long. We went to the harbour afterwards. Stockholm is bordered by the Baltic Sea and Lake Mälaren, and it looked gorgeous as the sun shone on the water.

We went into a park that had an ornate door. We also walked along the water. We ended up in a square with various shops. I bought *lángos* (fried bread common in Hungary), but there were shrimps on it. We don't have that topping in Hungary, so I was surprised. We went and looked at Skansen where they have historical houses, farms, animals, orchards, and gardens.

We boarded the train to Uppsala after that. There were a lot of bicycles at the train station in Uppsala. Of course, there were a lot of mopeds too. We also went down to the city and it was a beautiful town. I also found an ICA shop here and we laughed about it again. We visited the City Forest (Stadsskogen), Uppsala Cathedral (the tallest church in Scandinavia), and Uppsala castle. Unfortunately, we had to go back to Hungary the next day.

Later, I began to chat on Facebook with other Jenny fans: Melinda, Zsuzsi, and Berta. We learned that Jenny would be performing again in Hungary on the 25th of November 2017 at the Total Dance Festival. I bought tickets with the girls right away.

On that great day, we arrived in Budapest by train. Berta was already waiting at the station. Then we went to the hotel. I put my luggage in the room and then we went directly to the arena. We passed through security, sat down on a bench, and waited.

We texted with Jessi to arrange a meeting with Jenny again. It was so exciting, but even then I did not think that we would be able to meet Jenny again. Jessi asked us to take a photo and send it to her. She sent a picture back of Jenny's bodyguard. Later, the bodyguard said hello and shook hands with everybody. We learned that after the show we were supposed to go to the side of the stage to meet Jenny.

The concert started with "Happy Nation," then "The Sign," "Don't Turn Around," "All That She Wants," and "Beautiful Life." It was very good! Jenny sang well and the dancers were very good too. Awesome to see her live again!

When the show was over, we went to the side of the stage where others joined us. We waited a while then we were invited to meet Jenny. She appeared and kindly greeted us and kissed everyone.

She made sure to talk to everybody. She took my hand and said, "Your hands are cold. Are you cold?" "Did she ask me what I am?" I thought. I was totally blocked with the excitement and all I said was "Okay." I could hardly speak, but I did.

I brought a photo from the first concert to this meeting and she signed it. Then we took a photo with her. Later, we took a group photo with everyone who was there. It was a memorable day for me because my birthday was on the 27th, so it was a gift for me and I was delighted. Jenny, I'm grateful and thank you for this experience!

I could not believe we met her again and did not have to wait as long the second time. I consider myself fortunate to have met her twice! I am grateful to Jenny for still singing and for helping us with her music during difficult days too! And, of course, thanks to Ace of Base as well!

"We have only one life, and you should live the way you want it and not the way others want it!" I hope I managed to bring you some enjoyment with these "live for today" stories from my life!

Ilona living for today: meeting Jenny at the Total Dance Festival (2017)

ABOUT THE AUTHOR: Ilona Major is a shop assistant from Hungary. She has a beautiful fifteen-year-old daughter named Jenny. Unfortunately, Ilona's mother passed away as a young woman and her biggest dream never came true: to see the sea. Ilona feels lucky because she has managed to see it several times, for example in Sweden, in the UK, and in Greece. Contact Ilona at majorilona27@freemail.hu.

I Saw The Sign...

by Cátia Santos

We were in October 2005…My life was changing so much that year. Some months back, my boyfriend and I, we broke up after seven years. I lost my job and got a new one in a completely different area. My emotions were like a roller coaster. I was hungry for adventure and I wanted to discover the world. And for the first time in years, I was feeling free!!!

A Saturday morning, I left home and took a direct flight to Brussels. I was anxious and excited at the same time. I was travelling alone to an unknown country to attend an international show that took place every year in Antwerp: The Night of the Proms.

I was ready to accomplish one of my biggest dreams: watching Ace of Base live. They would perform a few songs only, but it was something that I've dreamt about since I was thirteen years old.

For that big moment, I was carrying one handbag and a lot of expectations. Once on the airplane, when the flight attendant announced the landing in Bruxelles International Airport, my heart bounced! It was really happening! But still, I had a long way to my final destination in Antwerp. My next step was to find the railway station.

I was in Belgium, and French is one of the official languages. As a French speaker, I thought everybody there could speak it and that it would be quite easy to communicate, but I was wrong! Most of the people speak Flemish, and sometimes it was difficult to get information. When I asked for a ticket to Antwerp's Central Station at the ticket office, they almost sent me to Bruxelles' Central Station!!! But after overcoming these difficulties, I had a pleasant trip.

While I was looking out the window and enjoying the nice views, I couldn't stop dreaming about what was about to happen that night. I was also excited to finally have the chance to meet other Ace of Base fans in person.

Patrick was waiting for me in Antwerp. He's a Portuguese fan like me, but he lives in a different town. For that reason, we had never met each other before. But we were used to speaking on Messenger and on fan pages quite often. He arrived one day before me and attended the first Night of the Proms concert.

Once I got there, he started to tell me everything he had experienced. He had amazing stories. When he was visiting the town, he met Jonas in a music store and Jenny and her husband in a street café. He could not believe it… and neither did I. I was wondering why I didn't come earlier, especially when he told me about the big surprise at the end of the show when all the fans were invited to meet & greet the band. I was delighted… His words increased my excitement and anxiety. Even if I couldn't meet Ace of Base, watching them performing live was already a big moment to me. And that big moment finally happened!!!

When the doors of the arena opened, we all ran to get a good place in front of the stage—and we got it. At that time, my heart was beating louder and louder! The staff of the arena were impressed when they saw Portugal printed on the tickets. But we were not the only ones... Many people from the different countries came to Antwerp just to see Ace of Base! I remember Ray and Lily from the Netherlands, Jessi from Germany, and many more names I no longer remember.

But it was not an ordinary band, it was ACE OF BASE! Even without Linn, it was like a historic moment because it was the first time in years they were on tour (or sort of).

I can't remember which artist opened the show, but I remember that I enjoyed the performance of Safri Duo a lot! Combining electronic music with a symphonic orchestra gave an amazing effect. Donna Summer was great too. She was a huge disco music icon and it was fun to see her.

And the great moment arrived! I have no words to describe what I felt when I first saw them!! It was a like a daydream... They were standing in front of me for real and I couldn't believe it. They only performed two or three songs, but it was one of the greatest moments of my life. If we could stop time... I wished that moment could last forever, but unfortunately good things also come to an end!

I can't remember very well what happened after the show... Everything is a little bit blurred in my mind. I remember we tried to meet the band at the hotel, but it was unfruitful! There was no meeting that night. I was a little bit sad for that, but at the same time, I was ecstatic with everything that happened!!!

Even though it was a short performance, it was a big experience and it had a major effect on me. It was not only the show—the trip, the people that I met, the city—everything was very important to me!

When I came back home, I was no longer the same person. As I told in the beginning, I was living troubled times—and this experience changed everything. It washed away all the tears that I had cried and allowed me to see the world in a different perspective, like the song, "I saw the sign..." It was the sign that I was waiting for, and it opened up my eyes to start living in a happier way.

Cátia posing with Jenny after the Ace of Base Copenhagen concert (2007)

ABOUT THE AUTHOR: Cátia was born in Lisbon, Portugal and moved to Lausanne, Switzerland as a kid. Later, she returned to Portugal to finish her studies and begin work. Today, she works in the aviation industry. She also teaches Zumba. Cátia is a joyful person who loves to laugh, dance, and take walks in nature or close to the sea. In her free time, she practices agility training with one of her dogs. She loves animals, so she volunteers at a local shelter. "The Sign," "Beautiful Life," and "Give Me The Faith," are three of her top songs. You can contact her at: catiavsantos@gmail.com.

Make This Broken Angel Sing

by Pablo Patricio Cáceres Gómez

I don't know when the last time was, that last time I saw him. The last time I heard his voice and that look in his eyes, in his blue eyes. An unmistakable spark that can be seen in the eyes of all people, if you pay close attention. That spark of life; the soul. What disappears when people are not with us anymore but what continues beside us, even though we don't see it. That is what I have learned over the last few years.

Sometimes, life presents us with difficult situations. We believe that it messes with our existence, and maybe it's true. Or we simply believe that we are the only ones who are hurting, the only ones who are suffering. But this is a complete lie. We are millions in the world with different situations, different realities, different points of view. Hard situations are intrinsic to life. And so is suffering. And, of course, good and happy moments too. I remember speaking with my father about it years ago when we travelled to the capital city for my first study day at my university prep classes.

I imagine that he saw the fear in my face. I was really afraid! I have always been a nervous person, and this was no exception. He started to speak about this; about the problems and fears of life—that we are not the only ones. He told me how he felt in similar moments when he was young like me. He emphasized that in every bad moment there is an end, nothing is forever! That really calmed me, and he was right! By the time he returned home to our village, I had completely forgotten about my fear and nervousness.

That first study year was marvelous. My life changed a lot. I was studying in a city so much bigger than my village and getting used to driving my own life, knowing new people, and knowing the city! But the most important thing that year was the release of the third album by my favorite and beloved music band, Ace of Base. *Flowers* was the name of the album.

I remember walking downtown one day and stumbling upon Jenny Berggren! The lead singer of the band at the time was featured in a big picture display glued to the music shop showcase! She looked beautiful! The album and the first single were on sale. To find that shop was a real bit of luck! I was with my father too at that moment. I couldn't stop speaking to him about it. He listened patiently. I imagine how bored he felt, but he never showed me. I started to buy every CD that year, and the following years too.

Time passed and many things changed with it: the day-to-day tasks, the people, and above all, the relationships. It was common to see fights between my parents. My father began to worry about other things, about himself. Many times, I defended my mother from him and I strongly reproached him for his attitude and lack of concern for his other sons, my sister, and me. Those were difficult days.

Time kept going and everything got worse—until my father left the house one day and never returned. It was a strange situation. They say that all things have a good part and another bad part. This is a plausible example of that. My mother felt much calmer. And me too, thanks to that, but how I would have liked things to be different.

So many times, I felt a lot of anger towards my father. I could never understand an attitude like his. I tried to approach him but I felt resentment until the day he left. He never told us where he went.

Life has to continue and that's how it was. We all tried to carry on with our lives, my mother, my sister and I. I ran my race day by day. I continued my passions and my art. And I continued to love music, which is a great medicine for the soul.

I loved my favorite band more strongly. And I learned of a beautiful and unknown facet before me. Jenny singing extraordinary pop songs in Ace of Base was a facet we knew already. The new facet was to hear her singing church songs in a completely different style, a wonderful style. It was something totally different from her participation in the band. The first presentation of "Give Me The Faith" took place on TV next to Jakob, her boyfriend at the time. I must confess I was open-mouthed, speechless! What a song! And what a voice!

Throughout the years, I continued listening to and watching other presentations of her and this song. Her voice and interpretation grew more and more impressive with each new performance. A website called The Jenny Source published many other religious songs. The unparalleled sensation caused by that voice—so fragile and powerful at the same time— is incredible to me. A real wonder! My dream is to see her in person one day singing in that sublime style.

The years continued into an ordinary day during the month of August, a sunny but cold morning at the end of the month… It became a day for nothing ordinary. To be more exact, it was a day that I will never forget, but I would like to do just that. Forget it forever. Save it in the last drawer of a piece of furniture in the back of the house with a double or triple padlock. That morning, I was getting ready to go to work. Someone knocked on the door quickly and violently.

Who is knocking!? I hurried to open the door and saw two policemen standing with harsh and worried expressions on their faces.

"Are you Mr. Pablo Patricio?" one of them asked.
"Yes. What's going on?" I asked restless and nervous.

I never imagined the answer, nor did I think in the deepest part of my being...

"We have the mission to communicate to you and your family the sad news that your father suffered a stroke. He is unconscious in the hospital."

My first reaction was disbelief. A thousand ideas crossed through my mind in a second. The police continued talking, explaining which hospital he was in, and how the events had happened. I tried to understand the implications...

The first image that comes to mind is of my sister and me traveling to the capital city. The two of us alone without speaking a word, holding each other. Imagining our journey, wondering what we would find. We knew he was unconscious and on the verge of death. The second image I remember is asking the hospital staff about his real situation. There was nothing we could do. His death was imminent within the next few hours.

The next thing was even more terrible: to enter the room where he was, unconscious and intubated. I approached him. Seeing his face after almost ten years and in those conditions... It was not more than five minutes that we stood there next to him.

"Hear me, please! Wake up! Give a little signal that you know that we are here beside you now! Why did you do it?!" Of course nothing happened. I had a secret hope that he would react, in spite of the diagnosis from the doctors. But inevitably, their diagnosis was fulfilled. Around three in the morning, they told us that he had died. There was nothing to do. Time was over. He would never be more.

What comes next is something very difficult to remember or re-live: the process of removing the body from the morgue. Seeing it dead... but if you can rescue something from a situation like this, if it can be done, it was that my father was not there. That soul in his blue eyes was not there. There was only an inert body, a cold doll. If his soul was not there, where was he?

After the funeral, the hardest part came: accepting a situation like that. Being able to overcome the injustice of having lost him without talking to him before. Why did he leave and never return? How many times have I imagined seeing him appear again and being able to converse with him and returning to a relationship with him. But it never happened and it will never happen. Why did this have to happen? I felt anger for a long time and a deep sadness that I thought would never end.

I know that my father loved me. I have many good memories of him with me. I can remember all the memories from when I was small. That is why his absence will be something I will never understand. And I always thought that the greatest injustice was that he died that way, overnight, and without being able to reconcile with us. But it was like that and there is no going back.

I always imagined, and even dreamt, that one day he would return the same as the last time I saw him. When we spoke for the last time, sometime in 2004 or 2005, when I looked in his eyes for the last time—that moment will stay forever in my vision.

The people who knew him where he lived told me that he always remembered us. He talked to them about me. In fact, they all knew my name. They told him to look for us again. They said he came to my town more than once and watched from afar, but he never dared to speak to me. He was so close. If a little impulse in his mind had made him reach out, he would have been welcomed by us. A little initiative from him and things would have been different. But it depended on him. If I had known where he was...

"Give me the faith that moves the mountains
Mountains of sorrow and despair
Take me through journeys of redemption
Lord, make this broken angel sing"

It's incredible how the things you love can help you move forward, to overcome your problems, whether they are small or not. And it's incredible how destiny is—like the music that came to my life years ago when I was still a child. Music that continued throughout my later years and into my adult life, and which I love. I could not imagine that "Give Me The Faith," the song I had known for years (and one that Jenny Berggren later included on her solo album *My Story*), would help me see things from another point of view. A point of view that would finally help me overcome something as terrible as the loss of a loved one. To find a loved one, even though he is not physically next to me.

With songs like "The Sky Proclaims Your Glory," and many more, Jenny unknowingly helped me understand that another world exists that we do not realize. Why look at the ground if we can look to the sky?

I think "Give Me The Faith" is the most important song of Jenny's in my life. It's as if she were a heavenly and positive entity come to give me a hand and get me out of everything bad. As if she was teaching me that there is something more apart from the earthly, "Make this broken angel sing."

Later and coincidentally, my best friend Adrienn created a beautiful piano version of this song and I made a video for it. It was a beautiful experience. To work on it helped me a lot again. My dear friend knows it too, but this is another story.

I remember a starry night with my father looking at the sky and talking about what is beyond the stars, if the universe has an end as far as it goes. One of the possibilities we thought of was that the deceased people, their spirits live in worlds beyond all that. Now he knows. Maybe one day he will tell me.

More than once, I have dreamt of my father and he always looks happy, except once when he came to my house with a worried face, as if he wanted to tell me something. The next day I understood because we received the news that my grandmother—his mother—was seriously ill in the hospital. I had no way of knowing before that. Then I understood that he is always close. So, I am sorry, why should I continue crying then? It is unnecessary.

We continue in this world and each one has a mission that must end, and after that, it is inevitable that our time to die will come. And who knows, maybe we will continue our being in another place. And I will finally be able to talk with him, with my father.

God is wise. He always puts us on the road to the things that can help us when we need them. He was able to send me an angel that, with her singing, helped me realize that my father is with me and always will be. That angel is Jenny, Jenny Berggren.

Pablo at home, with band photos and one of his drawings on the back wall

ABOUT THE AUTHOR: Pablo was born in the autumn of 1980 in a city called Rancagua in Chile. He was introduced to Ace of Base at twelve, and the band's music has followed him through life's ups and downs ever since. When he is not working as a bodega boss in a car repair shop, he is drawing comics and other creations—or posting to his two Facebook groups: *Universe Ace of Base* and *Jenny Berggren, A Natural Superstar*. His fan name is Pablo Patricio Berggren and that's the name you can search for on Facebook.

Bedu's Top Three

by Sci "Bedu" Sumantri

"Air of Love":

It is simple and uncomplicated. Jenny tells it the way it was for her. I think she poured out her experiences when she was no longer a part of her band, when she tried new air. When she had created some songs, she could already feel the air of love.

This song encourages us and shows us how to get out of a prolonged distress. The air of love is still available cleanly above us. Just stay, whether we want to feel it or not. This is my favorite song. Its tone is very well arranged and neat. Powerful when singing it. It is challenging and makes us think deeply. Thank you Jenny for this song.

"Dying To Stay Alive":

Have you ever been walking and when you stop, your mind is running to remember what you have done? Remembering what you have accomplished? Remembering what you have failed to achieve? But now you're standing on your highway. Your success is a result of your hard work. Then what are you gonna do...? Take a walk? Do a dance? Maybe sing. Maybe scream too. I did. Maybe you did too.

We all have done the hard work to stay alive. This is what I think Jenny wants to express in this song. That it was so difficult to get out of the the Ace of Base shadows. She was so dying to survive, to stay alive beyond Ace of Base. The beat and tone of this song is amazing, so alive.

"Living In A Circus":

Try to remember and review who we have been in our lives. Try to remember what we can do, what we have done. Did we take lots of action? Did we see the colors from morning till night? Did we just see it—or make color as well? What color did we make? Is your color against the nature colors? Is it fighting the blue? Or is it clear?

We are not only spectators and lovers, but we are also players in our respective arena. What are you doing in your arena? Making a lot of money? Singing? Selling food? Taking care of your parents? Advising your sisters and brothers? Raising a child? Or taking care of yourself? Life is a circus arena with you. This song from Jenny is making us aware of what we are doing in life.

Bedu at home showing one of his prized cassette tapes (2017)

ABOUT THE AUTHOR: Bedu is a fan from Samarinda City, Indonesia who enjoys listening to music, analyzing songs, and singing karaoke in the Smule singing app. His Smule username is EDD_EDU. Join him there if you want to sing a duet with him or hear him sing his favorite tracks.

Finding Someone in the Loneliness

by Adrienn Döbrössi

My story starts in 1994 at that moment when "The Sign" became a hit in Hungary. I was eleven years old. This was the first time I had heard about this Scandinavian group called Ace of Base and about Jenny Berggren. When I first saw her, I felt something words can't describe; she was something special. I was a child, only eleven years old, so I could be a real fan. I could adore her the way only a child can adore someone. I miss those feelings nowadays. They were so clear and innocent.

I grew up with rock music and reggae. I didn't know anything about pop. Discovering pop music with Ace of Base was something new for me. To be honest, I never liked pop music and I don't like it much now too, except for Ace of Base and Jenny. So it was weird to me that I started to be interested in them. I felt something I can't describe; some connection, but I didn't know the reason.

The year of 1994, before I heard "The Sign," was a real change in my life. I discovered Art. Grandma, who raised me, had brought me to exhibitions since I was three years old. We went to theatres and to concerts, so I got to know art very early. But that year, I discovered art inside my soul. It was a real miracle because I couldn't draw. Absolutely nothing. My art teacher gave me a two for the year and only because with a one, I would need to repeat the class. And

113

this was so until 1994—the magical year when I was brought to the hospital and needed to spend a week there.

You think that's bad. I thought the same, but this was what I needed. I was so bored in those years; there was no internet or smart phones, nothing. So, I asked the nurse to give me paper to draw. She got angry because little children just scribbled on the papers and they needed to throw them away. She yelled at me that if I did the same with the paper, I would be in big trouble. I was really scared. But something happened when I started to draw on the paper she gave me. I started to see lights and shadows. And I drew a perfect lion from the Lion King movie. I couldn't believe that I really could draw it. Neither would my art teacher.

The next time I went back to art class, we needed to draw a grape. I drew it and showed it to my teacher. He said only one thing, "Now I will show you shadowing." He believed I drew it without question. I didn't understand. After school, I asked him why and he said, "I saw what was inside you. I just waited until it came out, and now it did."

Step by step, I realized that I can draw, and with it, I wanted to draw Jenny. Never ask me why. I guess I don't know the answer even nowadays for this question. I started to draw, and because of Jenny, I started to learn to draw portraits. The only reason for this was simple: I wanted to draw her. After a couple of months, when I realized that I really could draw, I wanted to draw her.

My first drawing wasn't Jenny, it was Jonas. It's easier to draw a man than a woman, especially such a beautiful woman as Jenny. I think all fans would agree with me, but I mean beautiful in an artist's eyes. The two sides of her face are nearly the same. This is what our eyes see as beautiful. A little secret from drawing.

Anyway, I wanted to draw her and I tried again and again. What I didn't know was that this would take more than ten years of my life. But finally, I could draw her. You can say it's not a big success. But ask yourself, would I have learned to draw the hardest part of art without her? The answer is no. I became known because of her, and because of the picture that I drew of her. So thanks to Jenny, I became an artist. I grew up with her music and voice. She inspired me a lot in my life and in my art. A little piece of my soul tried to become like her.

When I got older, we were dancing to the band's music in discos, listening to them at parties, and everywhere, to be honest. We brought Ace of Base with us to school in our Walkmans. That was forbidden in those days, but we listened to it in the school garden. It was great to be a renegade.

Because I started to discover pop music, I found out that I love to dance. I went to a dance school, and later, I started to teach dance. I worked for a charity at a place where children who didn't have families lived. After a while, they started to tell me their stories, which were heartbreaking. But I loved to work there as a dance teacher. I could teach them not only the fun of dancing and how music can free your soul, but that life isn't as cruel as it seems to be in the beginning. I told them my story and that they can be everything they want to be. For them, it isn't the end, only the beginning. I loved them.

Because I loved Ace of Base, I loved Jenny, and because I loved Jenny, I loved pop music. Because I loved pop music, I learned to dance and could teach these children. Life is interesting, isn't it? You never know what comes into your life. Maybe it's a small thing like falling in love with music. But it brings you to a road where you can find a way to help others.

I grew up with a lot of friends, but my closest ones lived in broken families. One friend's father was an alcoholic who beat his family. My other friend's father did the same. One night, my friend's father broke his own son's hand and leg. My other friend's mother was also an alcoholic. I had another friend whose parents divorced, but his father didn't take care of him, so he was alone through the whole day. So they spent most of their time with me and my Grandma because here they found peace, love, and a real home. My Grandma loved all my friends like they were her grandchildren. So helping other people who are in need came from inside me. I saw it my whole life and I always searched for ways to do it. And I could do it—because of music in my past and because of art in my present. How will I do it in my future? It's a question, but I will find a way. I know it.

After high school, I went to work. Life wasn't easy in Hungary in the '90s and at the beginning of 2000. I went to work at a factory. I hated it from the very first time. An artist's soul is free. It's not made for robot work, as we called it. But we had no other choice, our families needed us. I remember every day like it happened yesterday. I had a Discman and I was listening to Ace of Base every day to survive. But then a nice story happened. I was listening to *The Bridge*. My work partner asked what I was listening to. I told her it was Ace of Base and she said she didn't like it. I asked her, "Are you sure?" and I gave her my Discman. I had her listen to Jenny's song, "Experience Pearls." She was so amazed, she told me that she never heard anything else like this before. She said it was the most beautiful song she had ever heard. And she became a fan because of Jenny.

I was very popular in school. I had a lot of friends as a child and as an adult too. I love being around people who I love. But I didn't know the answer to the question that no one knows, which is, "Who are your real friends?" Life gave me the answer.

In 2004, the hell started in my life. It was a real cold January. It was Sunday. I went to sleep like every day. Everything was fine. Monday morning came and I felt that something was really wrong. I went to the doctor. I was at home for a week with hard stomach pains. But it ended after a week, so I went back to work. But then, after two days it started again. It would not stop. Neither Grandmother nor I knew what was happening.

I went from doctor to doctor, but everything was negative. They said I'm ok. I lost a lot of weight. I couldn't eat because of the pain. In May, I was brought to the hospital because I couldn't get out of bed. And after a thousand tests, they found out that I have Crohn's disease. I was only twenty-one years old. I didn't know what to do. I thought my life was over. When my life had just started, everything seemed to be over.

I had a fiancé and we wanted to buy a house. After six months, my fiancé couldn't take it anymore, so we broke up. I lost my house with his share too. Lost everything in a minute. Some of my friends left me because I couldn't go to parties whenever I wanted. It always depended on my situation and how I felt at the moment.

After two years, my body started to give up the fight against the illness. I was very sick. I had so much pain that the doctors gave me painkillers. They were so strong that I can't really remember eighteen months of my life. Every day it was worse. They brought me to the hospital again and the doctors said they were not so sure that they could save me. I was fighting for my life. Grandma and my Godmother came to the hospital every day. Then the nurses asked me, "Why don't your friends come?" And I realized at that moment that I had no friends anymore. I was fighting alone because everybody had left me.

The surgery went well. I came home from the hospital after a month. I knew that I must get up on my feet again, but how? The people who gave me power weren't around. I was so disappointed. And then one day, I was listening to music. It was Ace of Base, it was *Da Capo*. And that song "Remember the Words." That song described my life. The text, "When you're down on your knees and without a friend. Standing afraid at the very end. Back on your own lonely and lost again…" My heart broke into a thousand pieces. But I don't know why I continued to listen. And then that part came, "We go up we go down, but we never stop. We are going to work it until we drop. Moving along you're going to be on top. Don't be afraid you are not alone. Don't ever think you're on your own…" and I didn't feel lonely anymore. This song was my hymn that year.

At that moment, I had found someone in my loneliness. It was Jenny, and I know it's sad, but Jenny was the only one that I had at that time. I will be grateful forever for the power she gave me, for the fight, and with her I could win. With her voice and songs, I would recover and become the artist, as it was meant to be from the beginning.

I didn't go back to the factory. I was learning and became a graphic designer. Right now, I work for a publisher and I can do both my loves: designing books and drawing. I found new friends who are always beside me—even when I can't get up from the bed.

I also need to mention my best friend, who I met on Facebook. The most wonderful person I ever met. His name is Pablo Patricio Cáceres a.k.a Pablo Patricio Berggren. We met the first time in an Acer group on Facebook. I felt something, but I didn't know what it was back then. The first time, I had a feeling I had known him since long, long ago. He was there all the time when I needed someone to talk to. I remember in 2017, when my boyfriend left me, Pablo didn't let me alone, not even for a minute. We talked and talked for hours. He is the nicest person I have ever met. A real friend in good or bad times, no matter what.

His friendship is a real treasure for me. And he isn't scared when I have some crazy ideas. He is there. For example, I've played the piano since my childhood. Jenny's "Give Me The Faith" is deeply meaningful to me. We always listened to this song when someone who was important for us passed away. This song is a calming island in those moments where we could find peace. And the feeling came, that strong feeling that I wanted to play it on piano. Not only the original, but putting my feelings inside of it. I told Pablo I wanted to make a cover of it. It took three months. It was the first cover I ever made and there were times when I wanted to give up. Pablo was always there and helped me out from those deep dark holes I was in.

I finished the song, but something was missing. And I knew it was Pablo. He and I are a perfect team. So I asked him to make a video for it. He said yes immediately. And that video… So beautiful, so calming. Pablo caught the feelings that I had. And with his video, the song became full. Like a diamond when you find it. It's not shining. You know it's something special, but you need something more to let it be what it should be. You need to sand it. Pablo sanded it and made it shine. He gave sparkle to my diamond. And this moment is important to me because I realized that he isn't only my best friend, but also my soul mate. Someone who feels what I am feeling without saying a word.

Since those dark days, my life changed a lot. I found my two best friends here in Hungary, Szilvia Verestói and Hajnalka Kiss. Both are artists and we fight for each other. I not only take part in exhibitions but also organize them with my two best friends, or should I say sisters.

I found my way in life, what really makes me happy. But without Jenny, I wouldn't have had the power to stand up again. No, I never met her. I can't tell stories about how sweet she is, but I know because my friends who met her told me. But I can say that there was a time when Jenny was my guardian angel.

Adrienn's hand drawn portrait of Jenny based on a photo from 2010

ABOUT THE AUTHOR: Adrienn Döbrössi lives in the countryside of Hungary. She is a graphic designer and works for a publisher designing books. Her passion is art. She is a steampunk artist and a portrait artist at the same time. She loves history and is a big fan of the Victorian Era, which is why she became a steampunk artist.

My Life, My Story

by Berta Kovacs

I was born in Budapest on a Christmas morning. I spent my childhood with my parents and my sister in one of the outer districts of the city. I learned a trade, but as life would have it, I work in the post office. It's hard to earn my friendship, but once I open my soul, I am inclusive and honest. My feelings are deep, but certain mood fluctuations belong to my basic nature. That's me. I also really like to listen to music. Two of my favorite sayings are:

> *"When you're happy, you enjoy the music. But when you're sad, you understand the words."*

> *"Music expresses that which cannot be formulated. It guides you through many problems. Music is a remedy for your soul."*

And, certainly, there is truth in these because that's the way I feel in many cases.

I like to go to concerts and blog about the experiences. I started blogging because I like to write. I asked myself whether people might be interested in my everyday life? Fortunately, my friends enjoy reading my concert blogs. According to some people, I write my very own point of view.

Why Ace of Base? Why Jenny? Ace of Base exploded onto the public consciousness when I was in high school with hits like "All That She Wants," "Happy Nation," and "The Sign." I thought that they were excellent songs and the band members were very nice. When I was fifteen, I listened to a lot of these songs. I wrote the band's name in my notebook, in my textbooks, and even on the school bench. I could not wait to see the video clips of them on TV. I collected articles from *Popcorn* and *Bravo* and my room was full of posters. *The Bridge* was my favorite album. I listened to it day and night.

Unfortunately, I was the only fan in the school. There was no one else with whom I could talk to about the band. We did not have the internet or other places where I could get to know other fans. Unfortunately, my family was not crazy about them either.

I hung out with my friends, but somehow, I considered the band members to be friends as well, even though I knew that it was not really the case. Of course, I had a big dream and desire: to go to a concert and meet them in person. But was this possible?

It remained a dream for some time since Ace of Base never played a concert in Hungary. So, instead, I admired the video clips on TV. I read about them in music magazines. And I placed posters on my bedroom wall.

As the years went by, my dream to see them in concert remained. Then the chance arrived. By that time, Linn had left the band. And Jenny, who had started her solo career, brought the spirit of Ace of Base performances to her own concerts.

I learned by chance that Jenny was scheduled to visit Hungary (on the 6th of August 2016, exactly). I was so happy to hear this news. So for me, there was no question. I was going. I made the best decision of my life to attend this concert. August 6th is my name day. In Hungary, a name or two is written on each day of the calendar. And on August 6th, you will find my name. So for me it was a special gift.

I got to the concert site and spoke with other people who were there to see Jenny. We were going to watch Jenny's concert from the front row. It was a huge experience for me as an adult. It was good to sing "Happy Nation," "The Sign," "All That She Wants," and other songs. I felt like a young teen for the duration of the concert. To be able to watch the concert from the front row was a fantastic experience. I met another fan at the venue named Daniel and we both partied together during the concert. I was in my element.

Then we had the chance to meet Jenny after the concert. I needed a little help from Daniel because I cannot really speak English well. We took each other's photos with Jenny too. Jenny could tell that we enjoyed the concert. It was fantastic.

I asked her for autographs and photos. She was very nice, took my hand goodbye, then I thought, "I do not believe it. I never thought I would ever get to see Jenny singing live, and certainly not on my name day." This name day was the best one of my life.

Later, I found Jenny's official Facebook page and the Ace of Base Hungarian fans group, a group that has an international composition. I shared a few photos from the concert in Budapest. People liked them on Facebook and they saw how happy I was to be there.

I did not have to wait another twenty years to meet Jenny a second time, but only a year. This time, we visited the Total Dance Festival Circus. A friend of mine told me about it.

I got a ticket right away and, this time, I talked to two other fans before. They soon acquired a ticket and we just had to wait for the event, which was going to happen on November 25, 2017.

I was not headed to the concert alone. I waited for Ilona at the railway station and then I met Melinda and Zsuzsi at Vezér Square. From there, we went by bus to the venue where we met Daniel. At the entrance, we were checked properly by security. The boys had to go to a separate place from the girls. We waited for Daniel to enter so we could go in as a group.

Jenny was scheduled to play in the middle of the event. We watched the first performers and danced to the music and took photos. I was so excited, I could hardly watch the artists on stage. Then there was a pause. And, as we approached Jenny's time to perform, I became more and more excited.

Then came the long-awaited action: "Happy Nation," "The Sign," "Don't Turn Around," "All That She Wants," and "Beautiful Life." I tried to film the beginning, but you cannot record video and dance at the same time, so I quickly gave up. Mainly because I went there to enjoy the concert. And I enjoyed it. It was good to hear teen favorites again. It was good to sing the songs again and dance to them. I wrote in my Facebook timeline that it was good to be a young teen again, to scream aloud those songs that you sang back then.

It was also touching what she said before singing "Don't Turn Around." That there is only one life and that this is not the end. Life will continue in Heaven and she will see her father there. It moved me completely.

Then it was over, Jenny's performance. As I wrote before, I found different fan groups after the first concert. Through the groups, another fan arranged for us to meet with Jenny after the second concert. We were told where to go and we waited there. I was totally excited as we waited.

Everybody was warmly welcomed by Jenny. She said that we should move closer and introduce ourselves. I was wearing a shirt that Jessi had sent to me and it was signed by Jenny. Jenny saw this and had a good laugh, and I laughed too. She signed the photos that I took at last year's concert. Then we took another photo. As I met with Jenny, she hugged me, and I her. I thanked her for the experience and then we said goodbye.

We went back home since the rest of the show was not as interesting for us. I was already so excited after seeing Jenny's performance. And I certainly could not concentrate on the show after meeting her. I could not believe it happened again, meeting Jenny.

I rarely post group photos to Facebook, but I shared the picture and wrote the following text: "Wow, I do not believe it! A second time! I was young and a teen again! And the second time, I met Jenny too! My best party!"

And I think that Jenny is an extraordinary woman who is very kind to people without any conditions, even to people she has never met. It was a great influence on me. All this after admiring her for years only in pictures, posters, video clips—and then to meet her in person on my name day.

I had ordered a copy of her book and brought it to this concert. Jenny wrote in it that I was sweet. She later autographed a card and wrote that I was an old friend. I was touched by this completely because I was not sure if she remembered me from before.

Jenny had a great effect on me because she showed me that, yes, even purehearted people exist in this world. Or at least it is rare that a world-famous singer is so nice to fans. When I first met her, for example, as we talked, she graciously took my hand and we took a photo. She said to me how happy I looked and that was true. I was very happy.

Secondly, she was very nice to us fans. And what a pleasant surprise for me when the first time she saw me, she hugged me immediately (this is unfortunately not the custom here), then a warm feeling ran through my heart and my soul. It was good to be around her. Jenny is a fantastic person. I hope you can meet her too and experience the same thing.

This concert was a big turnaround for me because I was not alone in my love for Ace of Base anymore. I found other fans in Hungary. And it certainly changed things in me because I have since been in a less depressed mood. Not annoyed because of earlier minor things and not frustrated by those things now. So I try humor to approach things instead.

I regret not being able to meet the other members of Ace of Base. I would have liked to meet Linn, Jonas, and Ulf as well but I do not think this will become a reality.

Thanks to Jenny, because if she had not performed these concerts, my dream would never have come true. And my story would be unknown to you. Thanks for reading. I hope you enjoyed it.

Melinda, Zsuzsi, and Berta at the Total Dance Festival (2017)

ABOUT THE AUTHOR: Berta still calls Budapest home. In her spare time, she likes swimming and riding her bike. She loves animals and has a soft spot for the cat her parents own. She has been a friend of music since childhood and that's why she enjoys going to concerts. She also enjoys taking photos at music events and anywhere she is on the go. Her mother says she sings off key, but she likes to sing her favorite songs anyway. Outside of this, she also enjoys going to the theater. You can contact Berta at bertakovacs@gmail.com or on Facebook at facebook.com/bertakovacs.

I Need Your Voice to Free Me

by Magdalena Krawczak

I wonder if anyone will pay attention to my talk. Will my speech about the fear of the dark be interesting to anyone?

I'm trying to calm myself, thinking about a melody, which definitely doesn't fit in this space. I'm looking at the beautiful ceiling over my head while sitting in this large, baroque reading room. I can't help it. This place is too beautiful to let me concentrate on my notes. Pieces of paper lay on my knees (knees which are… slightly trembling). And I feel that with every second, my hands are more sweaty.

I should have been giving my talk for ten minutes, so it can happen any time now. But the previous lecturer is still talking, even though his time has run out.

I am looking at my wristwatch, trying to convince myself that its little burden bothers me more than the strange twist in my stomach. I broke the habit of wearing wristwatches a few years ago, but now I should be aware of every minute that goes by. And I should deliver my talk in fifteen minutes, not one second more.

The man with the double-long talk has finished. So now's my turn. I get up, take my notes (and tissues), and take my place in front of the reading room. I hope that my voice won't tremble:

"According to Halina Krukowska, night has a special meaning for romanticism. It symbolises the inner life of a human being and also its tools, useful to explore reality. The night-time 'opens hearts and thoughts,' gives an occasion for getting lost in the world of our imagination. It could be a liberating experience, but it can also turn into a trap. That's because the great darkness makes one feel extremely lonely and awakens in the mind a great fear. Jean Delumeau notices that fear as a motif was not present in European culture for centuries, mainly because it was misunderstood, taken for cowardice. But fear is a natural human reaction, which gives one's mind an impulse to take action..."

Life has an odd sense of humour. Or, it just wanted to make sure that I would be experienced enough to give this talk. Because one day earlier...

* * *

I looked outside the window with a mix of curiosity and anxiety in my heart. I had spent eight hours on a bus to get to Wrocław. I have taken this trip because the University of Wrocław is hosting a conference about the motif of the night present in the literature of romanticism. And I happen to be a PhD student whose duty it is to give a talk from time to time during these kind of events (but this is going to be the first one for me).

So I had spent hours on a bus... feeling like the Hobbits when they were leaving the Shire, except that my Ring of Power looked like a few overprinted pages.

Of course, the prospect of this trip is very promising. I am on my way to "the Polish Venice," or "the city of bridges" (and also "the city of dwarfs," but don't make me explain it right now). The city with a long and complicated history. It officially existed from the tenth century, then it served as a residence to the Polish Dukes of Silesia. A document of great historical importance was created not so far from here: one that included the first sentence written in the Polish language. Through the next (almost) ten centuries, Wrocław was under the reign of many foreign kings and powers, until the end of the Second World War. It is again full of Poles taking care of Polish art collections. The people and historical treasures had come to this post-German city mainly from Lviv: after the great exchange of population, which took place after the war.

But Wrocław is also the biggest city in western Poland. Doesn't it sound like a big challenge? For me—it does.

Frankly, I am quite familiar with being away from home. Just not far, far away. For a few years, I had been living on my own in a bigger city. But I had known that place since I was a child, visiting it from time to time. In my student years, I had changed flats three times. And I had lived with many different people, not always friendly ones.

I can recall nights when I was tired, anxious, even resigned—but I had a perfect solution for all these unwanted feelings. I remember very well some of these moments: lying in bed, watching the shadows on the ceiling, and putting earphones in my ears—waiting for the music to begin. Then it didn't matter that everything had changed again—that I felt lost and unsure—because I could close my eyes and focus on the familiar voices. Melodies that never failed to make me forget about reality.

Of course, when I'm talking about that magical music, I have in mind Ace of Base. For me, it all started in the summer of 1998 when the group played a short concert in Poland. I was watching it on TV, I may say, by accident. Listening to the well-known songs, looking at the charming lead singer, I was wondering if the name of the band was the one that I had seen on a cassette tape hidden on the shelf in the living room. It was, and that's how I discovered the debut album for myself. I fell for this music completely and for good.

From the beginning, it was Jenny who was my favourite: I was enchanted by her warm smile and that kindness in her eyes. But of course, I also fell in love with her voice—beautiful, full of an artistic depth. When there was a time after *Da Capo,* when I knew what she had done as an Ace of Base member, she started working more on her own. And I was so glad that there was still more to discover, even if she was doing covers or having concerts in churches. I mean, I loved recordings from these concerts—I remember that I was listening to the tracks from a specific one like it all was an album. It was wonderful to discover new qualities in Jenny's singing. But I still hoped for a real solo album, which she would release one day.

When *My Story* was released, I was in the final year of my philological studies, having just begun writing a thesis. I remember that I was wearing earphones whenever possible—I liked these new songs so much. Even when I was working, music helped me focus. Although I did my writing mostly with Beethoven's *Moonlight Sonata,* when it was about making notes, reading sources, or just getting to the library—it was Jenny's voice in my earphones.

Some time has gone by since then, but my music playlists haven't changed too much. Travelling to Wrocław, I had all the most important tracks in my phone—and the songs from *My Story* were among them. But suddenly, the view outside the window told me that now I must be aware of reality as much as I can—my bus stopped and I was about to get out.

Ok, so here I am. With Wrocław all over me.
But which way should I go now?

Standing at the real crossroads, I wasn't sure which way I would choose. It all looked so much easier on the maps I had studied at home. I was so focused on finding the right way, I barely noticed the nice neo-Gothic church standing around the next corner. And I had no idea that the impressive skyscraper in the distance is one of the best landmarks in the city. I was excited about this trip, of course. But I was also… a bit unsure since I was afraid of getting lost.

Go for it, they said, it would be fun, they said. Dear God, what was I thinking? Wait, is that a tram stop?

It was. Almost the right one. I boarded the tram and quickly learned it was going in the opposite direction (God bless all these nice people who told me that and advised me what to do). I got out of that tram and successfully caught the correct one. When I got to the street I was looking for, I thought that it could only be better from now on. And so it was: eventually, I found myself standing before the door of my hotel.

Victory. I made it! "Good morning, I have a reservation…"

"Good morning. Sadly, we had to delete your reservation. There is a serious breakdown in our plumbing. We need to relocate all our guests to other hotels."

Suddenly, my two bags felt heavier. *Are you kidding me?*

"The motel that we have chosen for you is cheap, so you won't spend more money on it. And it's also near the centre, just situated on the other side of the city. I will order a taxi for you so you can get to that motel without problems."

Beat of my heart...

"Please, rest for a while, the taxi will arrive soon."

...plays a new song inside.

Maybe it shouldn't make a big difference for me. After all, from the beginning I didn't have the best orientation. But actually, it was different; looking at the maps at home, I didn't pay attention to the other parts of the city. Now, all I had was a phone without Google Maps and I was about to be placed... somewhere.

The door creaked open. A middle-aged man with a small ponytail greeted the receptionist. She pointed at me. The taxi driver smiled and made a move as if he wanted to take a bag from me, but seeing my nervous smile, he stopped. Clutching all my belongings, I followed him to the car and got in.

The buildings and streets passed by in a blur as the taxi moved forward. I started to feel dizzy, so I closed my eyes. But only for a few seconds.

"Sightseeing or business?"
"I... I will give a talk tomorrow, at the university."

"Sounds serious. What is it about? The talk?"
"Literature, folklore in the nineteenth century."

"I see. But you should find some time for sightseeing. There's so much to see. You know, I was born here. Have spent all my life here—and I'm so happy about it. I can't imagine living anywhere else, even doing anything else. I hope you'll enjoy your visit."

We passed blocks of flats, then the driver turned onto a small street. We slowed down and then we stopped.

"Well, I'm excited, but also a little nervous now. I need to know where I am. And how do I get to the university?"

"Don't worry. We're not far from the city centre. Look straight ahead: behind that building there is a main street. You'll find the tram stop there. Take the one that goes… Maybe I should show you."

He took the map from the glove compartment and gave me the instructions that I needed. I managed to smile more sincerely. Then I heard him wish me good luck before I got out of the taxi…*Yeah, I will need it.*

I found the reception and completed the formalities. With my key in hand, I walked into a long corridor. It looked, well, like a cellar in my high school. The corridors were dark and it was surprisingly cold. I realized that I had to go upstairs to find the right corridor. In the almost complete darkness, I reached my room and closed the door with a long sigh of relief.

Luckily, the room looked nice. It was clean and full of sunlight. I dropped my bags on the floor and sat on the chair.

Maybe it won't be that bad. At least I have a place to sleep.

After a while, I left the motel. I wanted to take a look at the main street. The receptionist said it would take ten minutes of walking to reach the market square. But my only thought was that it wouldn't be wise to try. I could have gotten lost again—and I didn't have time for that. I needed to rest and get ready for the next day. I decided that I'd better take a walk somewhere near. And so I did.

I strolled through a quiet neighbourhood in search of a place where I could get something hot to drink.

When night arrived and the darkness was all around, I was back in my room. I was sitting on the bed, eating my porridge from home. It was really cold, but... thanks to that familiar taste of home, I felt more secure. I was sitting in silence, re-reading my notes for the conference when a sudden noise, made by a slamming door, startled me. Clearly, the motel had other visitors. And they weren't subtle.

I put my notes aside when I realized I had read the same words over and over again without taking in the meaning. My gaze went to the window—and to the moon, which was shining behind it. Since the list of things that I was sure about ran short recently, it was nice to realize that there's only one moon out there. It was almost like a looking at a familiar face.

My cold porridge was finished. And I wondered if this was why I felt like I had a big ice cube in my stomach. I got up to put the notes and my empty dinner bowl on the table. Then I looked at the door and, for the last time (the tenth, possibly), checked to see if it was closed.

I sat on the bed again and slowly laid down. I looked at the moon behind the window again and couldn't decide what was more disturbing: the noises or the silence.

I'll get no sleep.
Behind the door, someone walked by loudly. Then someone screamed.
I'll get no sleep.
And all those bloody pages, staring at me from the table.
I'll get no sleep.

Oh, you... you idiot. Of course you won't fall asleep, unless you do one thing.

Once again, I scrambled out of bed and reached for my bag. A few seconds later, I was holding my earphones. And after another few seconds, there was...

...the sound of Jenny's voice in my ears.

It was like a big hug. The one that I needed.

It turned out that my music player was stopped on "Spend This Night." Really. The tracks passed one by one. And with every minute, I felt more comfortable as the words and sounds calmed my mind. The consciousness was leaving me slowly, I only knew that...

I am the queen of confusion...
...under the pale moon.

* * *

I hear applause from my listeners in the reading room. My speech on fear is a success. I finished in fifteen minutes and managed not to stutter or lose breath in the meantime. Now everyone is invited to have dinner.

All the lecturers take a... strange little walk. It feels like a school trip, except that these are research scientists walking in pairs. And with almost every footstep, it becomes more difficult to pay attention to the conversations. As we walk through the market square, I don't know where to look first—at the colorful, charming buildings all around or at the impressive Gothic towers? Impressive, but also so modest in their simplicity.

Curiouser and curiouser—in that lovely, Gothic Wonderland.

Finally, we arrive at the Old Town Hall. Someone mentions that the restaurant in its cellar is one of the oldest in this part of Europe—and it happens to be the place where we are heading. It seems that the chance for sightseeing has already found me.

After about an hour, I find myself in the market square again, strolling in the crowd and looking at the colorful buildings on the other side of the Town Hall. I know that I should go back to the university, listen to the other lecturers. But I realize that... I gotta go—somewhere else. That I'd love to be aware of every minute that was left. That I want to see so much more of this place because maybe it's the only chance I will ever have.

Soon, I pass by the beautiful Gothic church and stroll slowly beside the river. Then I head to a cute, small, red bridge. I have faint idea where I am actually going, but I keep moving while looking at the two towers that captured my attention earlier.

Walking forward, then crossing the next bridge, I am still in doubt; maybe I should have stayed between all those talking heads. But after a short while, I am certain. There is no more appropriate place to be for a romanticism researcher than a beautiful, medieval cathedral (the oldest in the whole of Poland, let me add). And show me a romantic who likes to play according to the rules? I like the thought that Novalis would be proud of me. Well, I am actually proud that I managed to walk back from the cathedral island that evening and find the right tram to get to the motel one last time.

The next day was the time for... going home.

One more time, I had a chance to take a taxi. It was a different driver, but he was also a talkative man. "Have you enjoyed your visit? How was the motel? Last week I gave a ride to another guest. He said that it was so cold in his room at night." He continued, "Do you plan to visit Wrocław again? Oh, you need to come next year. The Afrykarium in the ZOO will be open. Have you heard about it? They have spent a great deal of money on it. Probably there will be a lot of tourists because of that place."

Surprisingly, I visited Wrocław that next year. My research project earned some money from the university, and I could choose what I wanted to do with it, so I came back to Wrocław to spend some time at libraries, but not only. It became clear to me that one needs a long time to discover all that Wrocław has to offer.

The funny thing is… that some tourists asked *ME* for directions. And I was able to guide them. Not because I had checked a map, but because I've been there before. And with every trip, my bag gets a bit heavier. This probably has something to do with the fact that I spend more time in Wrocław. And I have stayed in some really nice hotels there—with electronic door handles.

* * *

You think the story's over? No, now's the time to show you that life has a remarkably odd sense of humour.

A few years later, after my first brave attempts to discover Wrocław, I went there for a special purpose. I was about to discover that it is not only the city where it's hard to navigate your steps—but also the place where the music from the Berggren siblings sounds familiar, but exceptional. Jenny was scheduled to perform here.

At first, the concert was scheduled for Valentine's Day, but then it was cancelled. I thought that it sounded too good to be true—to see her on stage, not just recorded on a track.

But then, surprisingly, another event was planned—and in the middle of June I was travelling to Wrocław once again.

Would you believe it if I said that while going to the concert, I needed to pass by that cold, dark motel? As I said, someone up there has an odd sense of humour. But it became perfectly clear to me a few hours later when, after the show, I met Jenny herself... and she hugged me for real. Some part of me still can't believe it actually happened. I wanted to tell her, at least, how much her voice has meant to me all these years... but I found myself absolutely out of any words. That was definitely the most unbelievable experience I have ever had.

Romantics believe that every journey has a deeper meaning—that it helps the traveler get to know himself better, brings him the opportunity to find things that he is looking for, even unconsciously. That travelling always brings, hmm... pearls of experience.

Advertisements describe Wrocław as "The Meeting Place." And indeed, I have experienced some essential meetings here—also the ones with my own fears. And it is said that anything you want exists on the other side of your fear. Just bet you might win.

Magdalena meeting Jenny after the concert in Wrocław (2017)

ABOUT THE AUTHOR: Magdalena lives in Poland and has been hypnotised by Jenny Berggren's voice since 1998. She believes that the universe is made of stories—and she spends her days finding and telling them. But whenever words turn out to be unuseful, she tries to create something beautiful by taking photos or fighting with threads while knitting or cross-stitching. You'll find her on Instagram under the nick "ellenai30." Another internet gateway to her is an email address: theotherwoman87@gmail.com.

Magic Recaptured

by Jonason Keeton

My name is Jonason Keeton and I've been loving music by Ace of Base and Jenny since 1993. After first hearing "Waiting for Magic" as an import "Alternative" song that summer, I was hooked. Over the past years, a lot has changed in my life. I graduated college, have had a successful career, met my soulmate, and created a home for us. One thing that has been constant is my love of music. It brings people together and breaks all sorts of barriers. I listen to music in some way every single day. And Jenny's music makes me feel happy. I'll usually have something she sings on a playlist almost every time.

One major impact has been how connected Jenny has been specifically over the past year. I had not really considered the thought that I'd ever get to see her sing live. While I got to see Jonas and Ulf, it wasn't the same without Jenny or Linn there. When the announcement came up that she was going to do a show in Houston, Texas, I was thrilled. I didn't think a show in the United States would ever happen. I had lost quite a few connections with other Acers since the 1990s when I was active with my own Ace of Base web page, reading the forum posts, and enjoying what others had to say or create. The show's announcement not only brought back some old acquaintances, I started making new ones. I had forgotten just how much I enjoyed talking to others about the music.

When the time came for the concert to happen, we all got the sad news that Jenny's work visa was not approved. I know she had to be more disappointed than anyone. But instead of just cancelling my trip to Houston, I took a chance to go anyway. Sara had made arrangements to meet before the concert and was still going to hold that event. When that day arrived, I finally got to meet many old and new acquaintances and enjoyed getting to know everyone. I brought my partner with me, Dale, and he also got to know many others as well. He put up with me playing these same songs for over twenty years, but I know he definitely liked a lot of the music, too. To our surprise, Sara and Jenny arranged to have a Skype meeting. Knowing a few others in the music industry, I was so happy that an artist would take the time to meet up with fans, even under the unfortunate circumstances. Most would not do that.

Jenny was so nice and really interested in hearing from all of us. I felt awkwardly shy for some reason, but I enjoyed it very much. One thing I took away from that meeting is something I continue to celebrate today. Jenny had mentioned having champagne on Mondays. It was such a boring work day, and doing that made the day a little brighter. Almost without fail, I now have my own #ChampagneMondays each week. Besides having a drink, I also celebrate a mundane day. I've learned to appreciate the day more than I previously had. Who would ever look forward to a Monday? I do!

Shortly after that missed concert, I saw that Jenny had scheduled two shows in Florida—just an hour by plane for me. I quickly arranged to go to both. In Boca Raton, I met even more new people and truly consider many of them friends for life. That concert had some big names from the '80s and '90s that I also enjoyed seeing: Exposé, Nu Shooz, Stevie B and even Boy George with a powerful version of "Purple Rain." The biggest highlight was that we got to sing "Happy Birthday" to Jenny when she met us off stage.

No one had much time to rest since we all traveled the next day to St. Petersburg, Florida, for the second concert. That one was a blast, even with it raining. The setlist was almost identical, although I was really impressed with "Gimme! Gimme! Gimme!" and one of her original songs, "Dying to Stay Alive." The crowd definitely went wild when she performed "All That She Wants."

Jenny arranged to talk with us backstage, but we ended up also dancing and enjoying the moment. I have some slightly embarrassing yet prized videos and photos of us all dancing together. Another artist who I really liked walked by during our meet and I told him he also put on a great show. He just stared at me and walked on. I was insignificant to him. That made the time Jenny took to meet with us matter even more.

When the Florida shows were done, one more came up. In early summertime 2017, there was one more show in Chicago. Here, Jenny was the main event. I met a few new friends once more, and we got a more formal meet & greet set up. Jenny remembered both me and Dale from the other concerts.

I also got a very interesting story. I had brought so many items I thought I would want to get signed, but I opted to have just one. It was a poster of *The Bridge* from the "Beautiful Life" maxi single. When Jenny saw it, her eyes lit up and she told us about how that black thing behind her shirt was a clip they completely forgot to edit out of the finished product. I don't think anyone else knew what that was or had ever known it was mistakenly left in there. Dale also got a photo signed, so we both had things to frame back home.

We were expecting La Bouche to start first, but they had some delays getting to the venue. As a result, Jenny was first up! I think a lot of us were caught off guard, but it ended up being a blessing.

Jenny came out in a sparkling silver jacket with a sparkling black outfit. She looked phenomenal.

We had a real treat with getting a medley of "Cruel Summer," "Wheel of Fortune," "Lucky Love," and "Life Is A Flower." That was new to this set for the US shows. We even got to see Jakob rock out to "Never Gonna Say I'm Sorry." I was always fond of the Rock version on the single and was very happy to hear that version live. She ended with "Beautiful Life" in time to also enjoy La Bouche. We enjoyed the concert immensely. She puts on one fantastic show!

So how do three concerts and a missed fourth one have a profound impact on me? I rediscovered friends from the past, made so many new ones, and realized how genuinely caring Jenny is for her fans. I now enjoy Mondays almost the most and am looking forward to meeting so many other Acers in Germany in 2018. Beyond that, I'll still be listening to the music—and have just that greater appreciation for Jenny's work, thanks to her taking the time and effort to interact with all of us.

Jon at the meet & greet in Boca Raton, Florida on Jenny's birthday (2017)

ABOUT THE AUTHOR: Jonason Keeton is from Atlanta, Georgia, United States and has worked in the banking software industry for more than twenty years. He originally created the Ace of Base Pix Page in late 1994 when few online websites were available. Besides listening to Jenny's and Ace of Base's music, he loves taking pictures, videos, and creating travel journals. A perfect day could simply be hanging out with friends and family. An avid globetrotter, he makes time to see new places and take in different cultures. He particularly enjoys going to Québec, Iceland, and New Zealand. He publishes videos of his travels online on YouTube (jonasonkeeton) and posts samples of his photography on Instagram (@jonasonkeeton). You can reach him at jonasonkeeton@gmail.com.

Believe in Your Dream

by Lily Tijssen

She never thought that one melody could change her life... forever.

It was a rainy October back in 1993 in her grey world, and she was about to give up. She never liked the life she was living. Her mother left her when she was six. Her father was sick for years. And she had to continue her life in an environment where she never felt accepted. She spent her days with tears, asking "Why, why me? Why should it be like this?"

She never dared to dream, but at thirteen years old, she thought about the ways to change the life she was living. Her life wasn't fair. "It's enough," she thought, "enough of being alone and lonely, no friends, no family who care, no future." She felt so alone and lonely, but how to change? The only answer was "give up" because she thought that everything was so dark.

She never listened to music—until that day in October. She turned on the radio, and suddenly, she heard somebody saying her name and dedicating a song to her with a message: "Never give up."

When she listened to that sound—the flute, the voices, the melody—suddenly something came into her veins. She could not describe how she felt. She had no idea what that was! What song was that? Who sang that song? It mesmerized her! And when the song stopped, she found out it was "All That She Wants" by Ace of Base.

From that moment, things changed. But how can a song make a thirteen-year-old girl without hope, without a dream, and about to give up turn her life around? She became a dreamer, continuing her life with faith. She began to pursue a dream—that someday she could meet Ace of Base, so she started trying to make it possible.

Years went by as she lived day by day, and still so much pain she had to deal with. She had a job and lived an everyday routine, meanwhile she spent time looking for information on finding work abroad. She lost her father when she was twenty-two, and from that moment she wanted to run away. She was so down, and nobody loved her like her dad, so she decided to leave the city where she grew up just to forget about the pain with all memories her dad left her. But where? Her father told her before he passed away, "Go wherever you want to go. Listen to your heart... Just pursue your dream."

She wanted to reach her dream to see her idols, her favorite band, so she decided to go abroad. She thought maybe going abroad could change her life. Maybe she would find a job that she could enjoy, but most of all, it was about a dream to see and meet the band in person abroad, somewhere in Europe!

She had been influenced by the message from the Swedish band she was in love with. All that music contained a good message. Songs like "Beautiful Life," "Ravine," "Young and Proud," "Don't Go Away," "I Pray," and "Beautiful Morning" kept encouraging her to stay positive and enjoy life. The songs gave her positive vibes to enjoy life and to never give up.

Even she herself thought her dream was impossible because there was no way she could afford it. She needed a lot of money to go to Europe. She tried to do what she could. She saved for years and, by the grace of God, she was able to save enough. One opportunity gave her the chance. Her close friend was planning to go to the Netherlands as an au pair. "What is an au pair??" She had no idea, but she found out it was the only way she could go to Europe. So she applied to that job and was hired. She now had the opportunity to fly to the Netherlands and stay for a year!

And the journey of living in the Netherlands had begun. She stayed for a year with a host family, working with their kids, and taking Dutch lessons. But it was not as easy as it seemed. She had to leave everything she knew behind. And being in the cold was hard to take. She missed home, but she kept believing that everything was going to be okay.

Living in Europe was a big change for her. Everything was different: the culture, the foods, the environment, the languages... When she felt homesick and when there was nothing she could do with so many ups and downs, she remembered the song saying, "Just remember the words. You are never on your own. You're not alone." Music like "Remember The Words," "Give Me The Faith," and "All Hope" helped her keep focus. And her faith helped her survive. She talked to God every day, a God who hears her prayers.

In the summer of 2007, she went to Sweden. A dream country she wanted to visit because that girl really wanted to meet her: Jenny, the one who always sent all the positive energy to the girl through the songs she sang. And after fourteen years of waiting, the girl's dream finally came true. That girl is me, Lily. And I was finally able to meet Jenny Berggren.

I heard from Jessi that Jenny was going to hold a lecture in Gothenburg, so I planned to be in the city that week. And I made a plan together with Anita, Jessi, and Anja to see each other there.

The first concert was on Björkö, an island north of the city. That was the very first time I met Jenny. I was at the church and somebody came up to me and asked, "Hey, what are you doing here?" (because I am Asian and it's odd to see me around the church). So I told him, "Listen… I came far away from Indonesia to see Jenny Berggren, so I will wait here until she arrives." And the priest just smiled. He had a bit of a shock when I told him I am from Indonesia!

Not long after, I saw some cars parking… And there she was!! Jenny! I trembled, ran to her, and asked: "Jenny??? Are you Jenny?? Oh my God, you are real!!!!" Jenny answered, "Yes, I am! But are you okay??" She gave me her hands and we walked inside the church. When the lecture began, I was sitting in the front row. Jenny started her lecture and said, "I have a special guest who came from Indonesia!" And she pointed at me!

After the show ended, I wanted to talk to Jenny and give her a letter and a gift that I had kept for many years. I had no idea where she was after the show, but I was able to find her again. We talked and took some pictures.

I gave Jenny a necklace, which she wore at the soundcheck for a second lecture in Gothenburg the next day. That second day was more relaxing. And she wrote me a message on the lecture agenda: "Lily, thank you for coming, big Love!" Those moments, I will never forget for the rest of my life.

And in November 2007, it was unexpected that Ace of Base would hold a concert in Copenhagen. I went there and was able to meet three of the band members. And Jenny still remembered me. Amazing! I was able to tell Jenny how I loved her so much and how thankful I was for the songs. I was about to cry and she hugged me with love!

It was a miracle how it happened. Because it seemed to be impossible! I couldn't believe it.

"Years go by and with it comes oh-so-many changes...." And when I think back about all those times, I smile when I see how my life has changed over the years. The girl I was became the woman I am today—a woman with a new life. I never thought I would stay forever in the Netherlands, but after I met Danny in the summer of 2009, it was love at first sight. We spent time together and decided to get married. Danny took me everywhere, to places I had never been before, and even to see Jenny again. He always supports me.

Danny and I built a family together. We have two kids and a furry baby now. My life is complete. It's amazing how one song changed my life forever! If it weren't for Ace of Base, I would have never dared to dream of seeing the world.

This story is based on my life experience and I want to thank all the people who have helped me reach my dream, who made it possible. You know who you are. And to Jenny Berggren: thank you so much for everything you have done—and for still keeping Ace of Base alive today. I love you so much.

Danny and Lily meeting Jenny in Oberhausen (2017)

ABOUT THE AUTHOR: Lily lives in The Netherlands together with her husband Danny, their boys Samuel and Julian, and their lovely dog Loempie. Lily loves spending time with her family and traveling whenever they can. When she listens to music, Ace of Base is always on her playlist and the boys like to dance to "All That She Wants" and "The Sign." Her motto is: "Enjoy life as much as you can, you only live once!" You can contact Lily via Facebook: facebook.com/5351L14, email: herrens_sanning@yahoo.se, or on Instagram: @lilytijssen.

Photos: Global Meet & Greets

Jessi, Anja, Jenny, Michael, Nancy, Carole and Ileana during the meet &
greet in Wiesbaden, Germany (May 2018)

Nathalie, Simon, and Anna meeting Jenny after one of the performances with The ABBA Orchestra in Sweden (2007)

Dave, Anja, Jenny, Jessi and Wassim wearing the Ace-ring during the meet & greet in London, UK (April 2018)

Sara together with Jenny, Jakob, and the backing singers Annika and Kerstin during the meet & greet in Boca Raton, Florida, USA (2017)

Jenny and Italian Acer Rocco joking during the meet & greet in Oberhausen, Germany (August 2017)

South American Acers Raphael and Vanessa with Jenny during the meet & greet in Lima, Peru (2017)

Acers from all around the world during the meet & greet in London, UK (April 2018)

US Acers during the meet & greet in Chicago, USA (2017)

Ace of Base Is in My Mind

by Daisy van Vugt

Dear fellow Acers, I'd like to share in short my fan story of when and why I became a fan of Ace of Base. I first heard of Ace of Base when "All That She Wants" came out. At the time, I was eleven years old. In 1993, I bought my first CD with my own money: a greatest hits CD with "All That She Wants" on it. From then on, I couldn't get the song out of my head. Later on, I bought *Happy Nation (U.S. Version)*.

When *The Bridge* was released, my father bought a copy without telling me. He put the CD in the player when I wasn't watching. So at first, I thought I was listening to the radio, and I said: "Hey, I don't know this song. It sounds very much like Ace of Base!" The next track came on and it still sounded much like Ace of Base… Then I finally got the clue, and I was just over the moon, so happy and surprised! That's when I started to collect everything there was to be found of the band. And nowadays, I have a great collection of CDs, as well as some vinyl, and a box full of magazine and newspaper articles (mostly Dutch and German).

Beautiful Life

It's hard to pick one favourite song, but if I have to choose, it would be "Beautiful Life" from the second album *The Bridge*, because of the positive message it conveys. As a child, whenever I felt down or was

159

worried about something, I would listen to this song and it would cheer me up and make me feel happy again. This song taught me to always look at the positive things in life and appreciate the little things that make life worthwhile. My favourite part of the lyrics is:

"Take a walk in the park when you feel down
There's so many things there that's gonna lift you up
See the nature in bloom, a laughing child
Such a dream, oh oh oh
It's a beautiful life..."

Acer friends

I've known two other Acers for many years now: Ric and Lily. Over the years, they became very good friends of mine.

Ric and I got to know each other on an internet forum, and after corresponding for awhile, we met in person in October 2003. Since then, we have become very good friends in good and bad times. Because we've known each other for fifteen years now (by the end of 2018), we are planning to celebrate this sometime soon. One of our shared dreams is to visit Sweden, and especially Gothenburg (of course), the place where it all started for Ace of Base.

Lily was my Indonesian pen pal for years. I still have all her letters. She now lives in the Netherlands too, and we have met several times over the years. When I met her for the first time in Amsterdam, she gave me a gift—a beautiful Indonesian necklace. I appreciated the gift very much.

Nowadays, the world is a smaller place with the internet and social media, which makes it so much easier to search for Ace of Base-related stuff like videos of performances, to stay up to date about Jenny's schedule, and to come in contact with other Acers. The Ace of Base

World Chat on WhatsApp has really renewed my interest in Ace of Base and Jenny. And over the last year, I have been adding some new items to my collection again—the first ones in a long time.

Night of the Proms

I have met Jonas, Ulf, and Jenny once in Antwerp, Belgium, at the Night of the Proms in October 2005. I was there together with my very good friend Ric. It meant a lot to me to have the chance to finally meet my favourite band in person after all these years.

During the occasion, I was so impressed and overwhelmed by all of it, I found it hard to find the right words to talk to them. I do remember Ulf signing my copy of *Da Capo*. I said to him, "I have been a fan for over ten years." In response, he signed my copy of *Da Capo* with the words "Wow, 10 years!" Whenever I read these words, it makes me smile and think of that moment.

Back to the '90s

The second time I met Jenny was at a "Back to the '90s" festival in Oberhausen on August 5th, 2017. It was only three months after giving birth to my second child, and it was my first weekend away again from my children. After the show, Jenny spoke with us for over an hour, and it was only just then I realised what a good-hearted and genuine person Jenny is. I am thankful for her not taking her fans for granted and really showing an interest in her fans.

I admire her very much for the fact that after all these years, she still enjoys travelling around the world singing her greatest hits. I would love to once hear her perform some songs from her own album *My Story*, from which "Dying to Stay Alive" is my favourite song. This year, I hope to meet Jenny again in August at the '90s festivals in Oberhausen and Nijmegen.

Ace of Base's influence can be felt all around the world up until today. Even the day I'm writing this, while enjoying a very nice holiday in France with my husband and children, we heard "The Sign" on the radio while eating lunch in a restaurant: "It's a beautiful life…..!"

Daisy with her Da Capo CD at a NOTP meet & greet (2005)

ABOUT THE AUTHOR: Daisy van Vugt lives in the Netherlands in Dordrecht, near Rotterdam. She has a degree in psychology. She is married to Marin and they have two children together, a son named Morris and a daughter named Emma.

Dreams, Struggles, and Hopes

by Roberto Chang

When living in Peru in the '90s and early 2000s, I always thought I wouldn't be able to fulfill my dream to meet the band or attend any of their concerts. I always felt jealous of the fans who lived in Europe and other parts of the planet where Ace of Base visited to promote themselves or perform. I always saw that opportunity as being so far from me, even though they were close to me in my heart with their music. But sometimes things change and dreams come true—one way or another.

In early 2016, I planned to spend Christmas in Peru with my family. "Why not give them a surprise visit?" I thought. I had not been able to spend Christmas with my family for ten years. So I bought my plane ticket early without telling them. You could say I love surprises. I was so excited and couldn't wait.

Time passed, and like I predicted, the surprise went over big with my family. We had a wonderful Christmas after ten years of me not being there. But I didn't know I was going to get a surprise too. It all happened during a dentist appointment: I was telling my dentist in Lima that I only had a few days left in the country because I had to return to the United States before the end of the year.

While the dental procedure was taking place, I had my mouth open all the way when I started hearing a commercial on the radio sitting on my dentist's counter. "The Sign" started playing and the announcement came along: "Like Entertainment presents for the first time in Lima, Peru, the founder and lead vocalist from Ace of Base, Jenny Berggren in concert, this January, Saturday 28th, 2017, Mango's Club in Lince. Tickets on sale now."

I wanted to jump out of the dentist seat, but I couldn't. So, I tried to yell and make a sign with my hand in the direction of the radio instead. I clearly remember my dentist telling me, "Hey Roberto, I guess you aren't going to attend the concert." I was like, *How in this world could this be happening?*" Thinking only because, obviously, I couldn't talk or yell while getting my dental procedure done. Finally a chance to see Jenny, my favorite band member from Ace of Base, in my own country was about to become a reality—and I wouldn't be able to attend!

I considered my options: spending two weeks in Peru for Christmas, then going back to work in the US, then seeing if there was a possibility to come back to Lima for just a week, then going back to the US again, and immediately embarking on a three-week trip to South America to visit Chile and Argentina in early February, which I had already been planning for months. I was going crazy trying to even think about all the logistics, but adding Jenny's concert in Lima was not an option.

I returned to the US in late December and began preparing for my trip to Chile and Argentina, visiting family in Chile, and going trekking to Southern Patagonia. I think this trip made up a bit for the fact that I couldn't attend Jenny's concert in Peru.

Back in the US in late February 2017, I watched some video footage from Jenny's concert in Peru. It was a full show. (I still was not letting it go, hahaha!) But some days passed and I, for some reason, googled Jenny Berggren's tour dates. And to my surprise, I saw an ad online saying "Jenny Berggren, '90s Dance Party Houston. Live in Concert." I jumped out of my sofa seat and started screaming, "What in this world!" I could not believe it at first, but then I said, "Finally, my chance to see Jenny could come true."

Later that night, after researching a bit, I found the Facebook page "Houston JAM" led by Sara West. I was so excited, I contacted her as soon as possible. And she replied to me also very fast. So it was March already, and I was starting to plan another trip. This time, destination Houston. I got plane tickets, hotel reservations, and even planned a tour of the city. I was feeling happy. But sad news came to my life once again.

My father got very sick and was diagnosed with stomach cancer in the second week of March. My mom and sister were hiding it from me at first, but then they let me know later. Gladly, after an MRI, doctors found out that it wasn't metastasized, so there was a bit of hope. By this time, I had almost everything arranged to see Jenny in Houston. But I was having mixed feelings, feeling guilty that I was going to make a trip to Houston and have a good time seeing Jenny. I remember talking to my mom about this, but she told me that it was not yet necessary for me to travel back and see my father because he knew I had just come back from the other trips.

If I'm not mistaken, in those days in late March, It was announced that Jenny was going to perform in Florida and it would be a double event: the LOTOS Music festival in Boca Raton on May 19th (which is Jenny's birthday) and the next day in St. Petersburg on May 20th, 2017. But my eyes were on the Houston JAM, specially that I was going to meet with other Acers for the first time. So I started to interact online with the Acers who would attend the Houston JAM. The experience was great, but rumors of a cancellation of Jenny's concert came a few days before the trip, and were finally confirmed the next day. I said to myself, "Oh no! Once again, this was my second chance. It can't be possible."

So even though other Acers were still attending the Houston JAM (thanks to the enthusiastic Sara who had so many cool things planned for this occasion), I had to cancel everything. Good thing the hotel was not paid in advance and I only lost my plane tickets. But they always say, "When a door closes, another door opens," so right away I started to see the possibility of attending both concerts in Florida.

This time, with the help of Kevin, my partner in crime, we started organizing our Florida trip with plane tickets, hotels, and concert VIP tickets. So the sadness of my second attempt to see Jenny practically disappeared with all the excitement of planning to see Jenny in Florida.

A few more weeks of work and we were already on the plane to Fort Lauderdale and then Boca Raton by car. I was so happy. And coordinating details with Sara from Houston and Jonason from Georgia was making the experience out of this world. We were all planning to stay at the same hotel, one close to the venue in Boca.

Finally, the day of Jenny's concert in Boca had arrived. And the chance to meet other Acers for the first time too. We had the pleasure of meeting Sara, Fulgencio, Vanessa, Jonason and Dale for the first time. A lot of excitement! Jon, Dale, Kev, and I had seats together on the VIP balcony. The VIP locations were a bit far from being the best places to see Jenny perform. It was still good, but a bit too far.

And here we go! Jenny appeared on stage with her "Intro" first and "Happy Nation" second. I was filming with my phone, but at the same time my heart was going crazy. I couldn't believe I was finally listening to Jenny sing Ace of Base songs live. My first dream come true: to be at Jenny's concert, which is the closest opportunity you can get to seeing Ace of Base. My second dream come true would happen after the concert: meeting with Jenny Berggren in person, and on her birthday. Can you imagine what else I could ask for? I would say this was a special occasion.

I remember being both nervous and excited in the moments before the meeting. But the moment arrived when Jenny walked out the door. We started to sing "Happy Birthday" briefly then Jenny began greeting us. I was in shock. I didn't know what to say. And suddenly, I just took her hand saying, "Nice to meet you, Jenny" and she smiled at me and said the same.

She started to pose for pictures and selfies, but the place was getting overcrowded fast cause other people outside our group started joining. So it was something very fast and a matter of effort to get a nice picture with Jenny and the dancers. I honestly felt that it all happened too fast, but it did finally happen in the end. And my heart was beating like crazy from the emotions of the night.

At breakfast in the morning, Kevin and I met with Jon and Sara. I was able to give them little surprise gifts from my previous trips to Argentina and Chile as an appreciation to them for meeting them for the first time. Right after, we started on the road to St. Pete. After around four hours of driving, we arrived in St. Petersburg for the second round of the LOTOS Festival at Jannus Live. Hotel check-in done and we were on a hunt for a nice restaurant to celebrate Kevin's birthday. And what better way to spend a birthday night than attending one of Jenny's concerts?

And what a concert! With a storm and heavy rain (I didn't see it coming, hahaha). Good thing we were all positioned right—center and in front of the stage. This allowed us to not get totally wet because of the rain. But it didn't matter. We were there for Jenny and she performed beautifully. This time Jakob couldn't join her on stage due to the rain, but we all met him later on.

After Jenny's performance, we all went backstage to a bit of a dark place, but still good for a brief encounter. Kevin skipped this one. (It was his birthday after all and he was a bit tired.) So this time, Jenny was all for ourselves! (Yes, hahaha!) As usual, she was always happy to meet her fans.

This time, I saw more of her human side, which is a greater experience. But I must say, she is the same person as an artist and as Jenny. The more time I was spending with Jenny, the more I got to feel her love, energy, and enthusiasm she has for us, her followers. Of course, more pictures were snapped, but what surprised me at that moment was that she was making us dance with her. And of course, we filmed that. She was hilarious, cheering us up the whole time.

After our time backstage, Jon, Dale, Fulgencio, and Vanessa called it a night. After saying goodbye to them, Sara, Joleen, Melissa and I went to a bar close to Jannus Live for a little after-party: some beers and a chat. A great way to finish a weekend full of new experiences. The next morning, almost everyone took their flights back to their cities. And besides seeing Jenny, I think this was the best part: meeting great people and making bonds that unite us forever.

After the excitement of this adventure and a return back home, some days had passed. A new announcement was made. Yes, Jenny was going to perform in Chicago almost a month later. This would be the perfect third time for me. But I was not sure if I could attend.

You know: a new trip, hotel, airplane ticket, ticket for the concert, etc. So after thoughtful consideration, I decided not to attend.

But inside myself, I was getting crazy thinking that this show in Chicago could be as good as the recent show Jenny did in Mexico. So there I was again, doing some research about airplane tickets to Chicago, looking for a hotel, and trying to stay in budget.

It was also tricky because I had a busy agenda. I had a U2 concert on June 20th and tickets on June 26th to see Tears for Fears and Daryl Hall & John Oates live, both in Washington DC. So after analyzing carefully, I found time to attend Jenny's show in Chicago on June 24th. That was the moment I went crazy, booking my plane ticket from Washington DC to Chicago, arriving early morning on June 24th and departing from Chicago the next morning to be back in time for the Monday concert. It was super crazy, but everything was starting to sync up with my plans.

A week after, I was already on the plane to Chicago. A new adventure was about to start. I arrived in Chicago early that morning. Right away, I took a train to downtown Chicago. I was able to visit the main attractions of the city: the Willis Tower and the 360 Building, the Chicago River, the Chicago Ferry, the Bean and the famous park. I took the train back to my hotel at the airport to refresh myself, change clothes, and get ready to meet the other Acers outside Joe's Live, the venue for the Summer Boom Boom event. I still can't believe I was able to manage my time to visit all those places in just a few hours and still get back in time to meet everyone.

Once I arrived at Joe's Live, I saw everyone there. There were new faces this time—and some old faces too. It was my pleasure to meet Sara, Jon, and Dale again. But this time, I got to meet Aldo, Carlos, Ritchie, Mike, Jeff, Bob, Sam, and the others too.

It felt surreal being there with a bigger group of fans. But I was enjoying every minute. I remember we were singing along to some Ace of Base songs. It reminded me of my early years in Peru singing with some friends just before many of the concerts I attended there. I have to say that we had a blast, thanks to Sara. She coordinated everything there, trying to make our experience the best. I don't have words to thank her more. She even booked a VIP table close to the stage just for us so the group could be all together. That is generosity right there. I feel proud to get to know her. But anyways, it was time to get in and to get ready for the good time.

Once inside the venue, we met Jenny right away close to the tables near the bar. To be honest, it was not the best place, but it didn't matter in the end 'cause we were meeting Jenny—and no matter where we were, we were just happy to be there.

For my third time meeting Jenny, this was way better than the previous two. I was able to talk more personally for a few minutes, have some CD covers autographed, and take pictures with her too. What I liked the best is that we were able to introduce ourselves and tell her more about us and what we do for living. I felt like we were friends with her. I don't know. It felt she was the artist we all love, but also somebody human (Of course she is, hahaha, 'cause we tend to idealize people, but she is always so natural—like a natural superstar, if you will).

We were all enjoying ourselves while waiting for La Bouche to arrive on stage. They were supposed to open the show, but they were late (due to a flight delay from Tennessee). So, suddenly plans changed, and there was Jenny looking gorgeous on stage, opening with "Happy Nation" with the crowd cheering for her. The place was packed. I feel pretty sure she was happy seeing the place packed. It was a great show! She took time to sing a medley of old Ace of Base hits, finishing with "Never Gonna Say I'm Sorry." I was so pleased that she made a complete show of almost fifty minutes, considering before I had only seen her for thirty-five minutes at the most. So this felt special.

What I also liked about the Chicago experience with Jenny is the fact that after the show, she came back from backstage to say goodbye to the Acer group. That surprised me, and I think all of us thought it was unexpected. She came out also with Bengt and Jakob. So we all got the chance to get more pictures with Jenny, including Jakob. I felt Jenny was feeling happy and thankful for the night, so there was me hugging Jenny again for the last time in 2017. All I can say is, I felt so happy. Not only for me, but for my fellow Acers too. We had the time of our lives.

But as many things in life, some chapters have to come to an end, and Chicago was almost ending. I started feeling tired after being awake since almost 4:00 a.m. that morning for my flight, then the tour in downtown Chicago, meeting Jenny, and the concert. Everyone had to return to their hotels and fly back the next day to their cities. It was 1:00 a.m. when I said goodbye to the others and made my way back to the hotel at the airport. A few hours later, I was on my plane seeing downtown Chicago from the air and thanking God for the opportunity to meet wonderful people—and for the opportunity to see Jenny for a third time. It was a blessing I will remember forever.

Back home in Virginia, after all the experiences from Chicago, new friendships and bonds were made, especially with the Acers who started to participate in the World Chat WhatsApp group created by Ritchie Stubbs. It was the best way to connect with new Acers from other parts of the world (and those Acers I had already met).

I know it can sound cliché to say, but time flies so fast and it was almost the end of August. I remember making a comment to my dear Acer friend Aldo that I didn't have Jenny's *My Story* CD. (How in the world didn't I have one, right? That's the same question I asked myself!) So I asked Aldo if he could make a digital copy of his CD because I had an idea for a secret project—making a vinyl version of Jenny's *My Story* album. Like a fan edition but with a limited amount of copies, due to the expense.

Usually, I am the one who likes to surprise people, but this time Aldo surprised me. Yeah, he really did. I asked for a digital copy, but he sent me an original second-hand copy of the *My Story* CD. (Thanks Aldo for that!) It was great to have the support of an Acer like Aldo since this was a secret project. He was so supportive and gave me suggestions to keep in mind. So all my ideas were almost in place.

After discussing my vinyl project with him, I started to plan how this could be a success and a well-made fan edition release. I have to say, the excitement was huge. Jenny's album is more than forty-eight minutes, so even at the early stages, I realized it would have to be a double vinyl to give space to the songs on each record.

I told Aldo that I would like to include three more songs (besides all the tracks from *My Story*), which were "Let Your Heart Be Mine" and two songs that I love so much from the *Så Mycket Bättre* CD: "Push Play" and "Come." I was tempted to include some songs in Swedish from Jenny, but I realized the English songs were more in-sync with the style of *My Story*. So it was going to be a Double Vinyl album with the first three sides for Jenny's *My Story* songs and the last side for the non-*My Story* songs.

Around the end of September, I saw an announcement on Facebook about the '90s Fest London 2018 concert with Jenny Berggren. I was amazed that Jenny was going to perform again at the same venue she did in April 2017. Since there were no more plans for Jenny to perform in the US during the second half of 2017 (and no clear events for 2018), I started to consider travelling to London to see Jenny again in 2018.

I had been to London before and had always wanted to come back (and also because I would like to visit my Aunt and my two cousins in London). So after careful consideration and discussion with Kevin, we agreed to organize a trip to London (and other countries, too). So as soon as the tickets went on sale, I bought them.

I sent a message to Live Entertainment and got a quick answer from Mantas, the "Guy" who is the director and who was bringing Jenny to London for the '90s Fest for a second year. So there I was again, organizing a trip to Europe just to see Jenny. As I told Jenny in person, "Jenny, it's all your fault!"

As soon as I told my high school friend Carmen I was going to London, we started to plan a reunion with two more friends from high school, Sara who lives in Amsterdam and Kathy who lives in Romania. We were thinking it was a great way to see each other after many years.

I couldn't ask for more: a trip with many great things to do, seeing Jenny, meeting friends from high school, visiting new places along the way, and meeting with other European Acers too. A dream trip? I think so.

At the same time, I was excited because December was getting closer and closer and it was time to travel to Lima, Peru, for Christmas again.

On this occasion, it was not a surprise trip like 2016. This time, I told my parents and sister I was coming. It was also planned way ahead because my father had been in cancer treatment with strong radiation and chemotherapy after his surgery. And I was literally crazy about giving him a huge hug and spending quality time with him and my family. I was so anxious to arrive in Lima.

I finally got to see my father, and to my surprise, he was so skinny and not looking the same as the past year. I had tears when I saw him, but at the same time, I felt quite happy to see him alive and recovering from those months of strong treatment. (I still cannot believe how a treatment can also almost kill you.) I was determined to enjoy every moment with him to the fullest because sometimes you don't know what could happen in the end.

At the same time, I was planning to make commemorative laminates with lanyards in Lima since it would be cheaper than making them in the US. These laminates were going to be given out to all the participants attending Jenny's meet & greet in London. Each one had a blank space that Jenny could sign. I thought it would be awesome to give the laminates away as a thank you for being there for Jenny. (I did share pictures of these laminates with Jessi and Mantas. They seemed pleased with the final outcome.)

The same graphic designers who made the laminates were working on the *My Story* covers to adjust them for the Double Vinyl. The back side was a complete redesign due to the modified track listing. Trying to make it look like a professional release, I used the A1, B1, C1, and D1 formats. The inner labels for each record were also custom designed. I tried to keep the design of the original. Quite a challenge, but doable. The final design was surprisingly great, as I wanted it. I tried not to miss any detail, at least visually. When I shared the previews with Aldo, he was impressed.

While at home with my family, I could see that my father was more enthusiastic, festive, and with more appetite. Probably also because we were there united. The four of us: me, my sister, mother, and father about to spend Christmas together. But a day before Christmas, my father started to feel bad and we got him to the emergency room. He had to stay there for the night. As soon as you hear such things, it's like your worst fears come back again: that something could go wrong again, but at the same time, we prayed to God and asked Him to take care of our father.

He spent the night at the hospital due to an intestinal obstruction (since he has no stomach, part of his intestines work as a small stomach). We didn't know if he was going to spend Christmas Eve hospitalized. I was praying for that not to happen, and finally, hours before Christmas Eve, he was released from the hospital after the doctors were able to clear the obstruction. We were able to take him home so that we could have Christmas Eve dinner together (but with some difficulty, considering my father's health). I still have those memories, seeing him feeling still weak but still trying to remain strong. I admire him for that. Later that night, we went to my grandmother's house for dinner with everyone, including my ninety-four-year-old grandmother. I was so thankful to God for letting me be there close to my family.

I still had more days to spend in Peru with my family before returning to the US. During those days, I found an old *Happy Nation* VHS video tape in PAL. I thought it was lost, so it was great to find it again. I also found another videotape with the twenty-five-year-old wedding anniversary of my parents, which we had not seen in more than fifteen years. (Who has a VHS player nowadays?) So I found a conversion service and made a transfer to DVD. One of the nights before I returned to the US, we all four watched it together in our living room. My father and mother got emotional. And I saw in my father's eyes, those nostalgic moments. And I could see how he was missing those days when he was younger and healthier. But we were there, all reunited and enjoying ourselves.

End of December and I was at the airport in Lima once again saying goodbye to my father, mother, and sister who went with me. My father was still recovering from the day he spent in the hospital but feeling a bit better. It's hard to leave your family behind, especially in these moments, but life has to continue. The good thing is, I had already booked another flight to come back to Peru in mid-March.

Back to the US for winter. I could say it was not a "Cruel Summer." It was a Cruel Winter, if you will. Super cold weather, the coldest in years, but that didn't stop us from continuing to plan our trip to Europe. I was also in touch with Jessi in regard to preparing for Jenny's show in London. And Wassim, another Acer from Australia, finally decided to join us in London too.

Two days before travelling back to Peru, my father started to feel sick. He went to the emergency room with lots of pain. He was released after two hours and went home with no signs of recovery. Then he was taken back to the emergency room because he was feeling worse. When I called my mother to see how he was feeling, my mother hid it from me, saying that he was already asleep. But when I called home, my sister told me he had been taken to the hospital again. I knew they were lying to me to protect me, but hiding it makes it worse. So I asked them not to lie to me or hide my father's condition. (I know it is hard when you are so far away, and I can understand them because they were afraid that I was going to get my blood pressure up.) I started to worry about my father. It was Sunday night and I was going to fly to Peru on Tuesday morning. I was becoming anxious. My father was going to have emergency surgery Monday evening, according to my mother. It was another obstruction, but it felt like they were not telling the whole truth. I felt like I just had to wait.

Tuesday morning came and I was at the airport waiting for my flight to Peru. Once inside the plane, as I usually do, I started listening to music. And this time, I was listening to Jenny's songs. "Give Me The Faith" is one of my favorites, and at times, it helps me go through hard moments. But on this occasion, it was time for "Going Home." I love the lyrics, but they were killing me this time when I was inside the plane trying to get home as soon as possible.

"For you my cherished one ....So won't you wait for me, wait for me I am coming for you ....Wait for me, wait for me ....As fast as I can ....Wait for me, wait for me ....Soon it will be over...... Wait for me, wait for me ....and I'll have you back again...."

It got to me and I just broke into tears inside that cold cabin plane, hoping that I would be able to see him alive.

Finally in Lima, my mom went to pick me up. She told me that my father was in the recovery room after surgery. But when I asked her to tell me the truth, she said that my father was not in good shape. That his situation was serious and complicated, and that they didn't want me to worry about him while travelling. But inside myself, I think I knew.

Once we got home from the airport, we got a call from the hospital saying that he was transferred to the Intensive Care Unit. I found out that he had a critical generalized infection and complications with his lungs. I was fearing the worst and started to pray, pray, and pray. I was not able to see my father until the next day when he finally got out of Intensive Care, but he was still in a difficult situation. At home, my sister and I broke down in tears.

But we had to be brave for my mom—and for my father to give him the support he needed.

Once at the hospital, it was heartbreaking to see him with all those tubes and drains and equipment connected to his body. I had to leave the room and cry alone outside because I didn't want my father to see me like that in front of him. I was supposed to show strength for him and I didn't want to disappoint him.

In the coming days, he got into a more stable condition, but he was still battling with a strong infection and a respiratory condition. As for me, I also had two important doctor appointments. I had two procedures scheduled for myself: one an endoscopy and another a colonoscopy. Both to check if there was something wrong with me due to the cancer history in our family. It turned out that the colonoscopy was good. No signs of lesions. But for my endoscopy, doctors found something irregular and they took biopsies from my stomach. I had to wait fifteen days for the results. But even though it could be a bad sign for me, I was not concerned about me, but about my father's health.

At the same time, I was trying to make time to create posters for the meet & greet with Jenny for the '90s London Fest. And I got them done in the end. I even got in touch with Jessi to show her.

Once again, it was time to come back to the US. I felt awful leaving my father in his condition still hospitalized. I literally took my luggage to the hospital and left for the airport from there. I told my father "keep fighting, keep fighting" and gave him a big hug. This time, I kept myself together and was brave to not cry in front of him, even though I was heartbroken inside. I told my father I was going to travel to Europe for this '90s Fest and I would try to come back to Peru and see him again after that, so he better get "better."

My mom and sister went to the airport with me because we wanted to be together a little longer. Once at the checkpoint, it was time to say goodbye. We all had tears in our eyes. We didn't know what was going to happen next. We just needed to be hopeful for my father.

Once back to the US, I tried to get myself together. Back to work and getting everything set for the European trip to see Jenny. The *My Story* Double Vinyl project was sent to production for seven units (fourteen vinyl records). It arrived in time—five days before departing for London.

On April 18th, we were ready for our European Adventure with everything packed: posters, laminates, lanyards, double vinyl albums, printed pictures to be signed, surprise gifts for Jenny, markers, gifts for my high school friends, and souvenir gifts for Dave, Anja, Mantas, Jessi, and Wassim. Yes, we were now on our flight to London from New York.

With jet lag on our shoulders, Kevin and I arrived in London on the morning of April 19th. After our hotel check in, we went to take the London Eye tour and the Thames River cruise tour. It was my second time in London, but for Kevin, this was his first visit. The weather in London was unusually warm and sunny. Rare for spring time, but we enjoyed every minute of it. It was good to be back.

To be connected with my father, I started to record short video messages showing him the places I was visiting to help distract him a bit from his hospital bed (yes, he was still in the hospital).

The next day, Kevin and I did more sightseeing. We went to the Changing of the Guard ceremony at Buckingham Palace early in the morning and it was amazing, but it was bittersweet because this day was also my father's birthday. How can I be in Europe so far away from my father on his birthday while he was in a hospital bed? I don't know how to answer this, but I know my father wouldn't want me to cancel because he was sick in Peru. I sent him a birthday video message from the Tower of London and called him. And he understood. I think parents, they always understand. But for me, that was the sour part of this trip in a way. I felt guilty inside, and that guilt went with me for almost the rest of the trip. But at least I was thinking of him the whole time and preparing those videos for him. When years pass, I will probably look back at these moments with nostalgia.

Friday night came along and it was time to meet with my dear Jessi and Anja from Germany for the first time. A long-awaited encounter after months of chatting online. Also we met with Mantas, Dave and David, and Leire and Hernan from Spain. It was surreal when we all met outside the O2 venue. It was a feeling of fellowship. Like I had already known everyone for a long time.

Before dinner, I gave out the presents I brought with me. There were some souvenirs from Peru for Mantas, Jessi, and Anja. Later, Dave and David joined us and I had something for them too. Aldo had a present for both Jessi and Anja, so I delivered one each to them: a black "Jenny cup" that changes to a picture when you pour hot water in it. They were surprised too. We also made plans for the next day, discussing more details of our meeting with Jenny and the final arrangements. Jessi, Kevin, and I were going to get All Access passes, so that was an excellent plus from Mantas. Dave also had a surprise gift for us. He gave a "Jenny Ace ring" to Jessi, Anja, and me. Meeting everyone for dinner (fish and chips, of course) was a great way to start our weekend experiences.

Saturday morning was "the day." Kevin and I had a planned an early tour to the British Houses of Parliament in central London to see inside the House of Commons and the House of Lords. (The tour was amazing, so much history.) After the tour, we went right back to our hotel near Canary Wharf because I was about to meet Wassim around noon. He was arriving from Italy, and we had planned to meet and visit prior to the meet & greet with Jenny.

Once at our hotel, we started to plan for the evening meeting. Wassim helped us with all the goodies we were planning to give to the Acers, including the posters and laminates with the lanyards. But he could not see Jenny's *My Story* Double Vinyl album because that would have ruined the surprise. I had them all wrapped in gift paper because he was going to get one. Minutes later, we were all going to the O2 Arena to meet the rest of the group. Excitement all around!

At the O2 Arena, we greeted each other again and were introduced to other participants too. Mantas greeted us, and pretty soon we were inside the Indigo at the O2 Arena. I was feeling very nervous, almost like the first meeting in Florida. I don't know why. Well, I guess because this time was going to be more personal. And because I was going to present a tribute to Jenny, which was her *My Story* in a Double Vinyl album version. This project was like my personal thanks to her for all the joy she gave me with her music from Ace of Base during all those years—and through her personal work with *My Story*. So, I didn't know how Jenny was going to react to that.

On the second floor, Jessi, Anja, and I arranged the table and cameras where Jenny was going to sit and probably sign our stuff. We also gave all the Acers their set of three posters so Jenny could sign those too. Minutes later, Jenny appeared.

Wow! That was the moment we were all waiting for. She was still recovering from pneumonia, so it was not that easy. She said she had to choose between going to see her kids and meeting us for a bit and she chose us. Jenny didn't want to disappoint us for sure. She even made us dance. I guess to break the ice between us and her—and to make it more fun.

Then Jenny asked us if we had some questions for her, and we did. For example, I asked her if she was working with new music and she responded yes and no. She always has some new ideas, but her producer was in Korea at that time. I also asked her if she had some plans to come to the US for any new shows and she responded that she had two dates planned for October. But nothing was confirmed at that moment. After a few more questions, it was time to start the one-on-one meetings with the Acers.

I think I asked Jessi if I could go first because I had stuff from other Acers who couldn't attend this event. So I started. And, boy, I was nervous. I started with Aldo's pictures he gave me to be signed by Jenny. (Carlos Santiago's pictures too, plus both their laminates signed.) After that, I gave Aldo's "Jenny cup" gift to Jenny. And I explained that she would have to pour hot water into it to see herself on it!

I started with my pictures from the St. Petersburg, Florida show. She said she looked good in Florida. I also brought two pictures from Chicago. Then I had surprise gifts for Jenny as well. With the help of my dear Jessi, I learned that Jenny's favorite color is purple and that she loves sunflowers. So I gave Jenny a Swarovski necklace sunflower pendant with a purple crystal, a purple sunflower plated bracelet, and an Amethyst purple crystal rhinestone sunflower pic brooch. When she opened the little box and saw them, her reaction was amazing. She got really surprised. (From time to time, I watch the videos back and I feel happy.)

But that was not all. For a moment, she thought it was all there was. But I said, "Well Jenny, there is something else that is very special from me to you too." I told her, "Only a few people have this, but I asked them not to open it until you open it." Jenny was getting intrigued, I could tell. "Nobody is supposed to open it before you do." Unexpectedly, Jenny said, "Well let's get everyone who has it closer to the table so we can all open it at the same time." I was thinking at that moment, *"Hmm, this is turning out way better than I had planned."* I didn't think about everyone opening it at the same time.

I was so looking forward to this surprise moment for months. So, yeah, moment of truth… Jenny opened it first to find out that it was her *My Story* album in a Double Vinyl version. Jenny couldn't believe it. I can still see her face in my mind. She started to open the gatefold and take a closer look. I asked her to take a look at the back cover and the selection I made for this release (adding "Let Your Heart Be Mine," "Push Play," and "Come" on the last side of the project). She smiled and asked Jessi if she knew about this. (Jessi didn't know because she was going to be surprised too, of course. Hahahaha!) Jessi, Dave, and Wazzi were all shocked and surprised. I think I did a good job in surprising everyone. It was like, "Mission accomplished!"

One of the things I remember the most was when Jenny said, "You should be my record company." I was like, "Should I?" Jenny also said, "Now we have an idea of what we can do." I told Jenny that I only made a limited release of seven copies because this is an expensive release. Jenny agreed, "It is expensive."

I asked Jenny to sign one copy dedicated to Aldo, who was the only Acer who knew about this, and one copy for me. Since I gave Jenny two copies, there was a moment where she really surprised me—when she asked me to sign the copy to her. I was like, "What?" Speechless. Then I was like, "Oh My God." And I did. I dedicated the album to her from me. That was so surreal to me. I felt so happy to do it. And when I finished signing it, Jenny said, "This copy is going to be the expensive one." I felt like I was in Heaven.

She then posed for the camera with Jessi, Dave, Wazzi, and me holding our copies of the *My Story* Double Vinyl for a group picture. It was the most amazing moment and a really great meet & greet so far...and we were just beginning the evening.

After this, I apologized to all for the longer time I took to present all these items. But I think the others understood. Right away, all the rest of the Acers had their time with Jenny too as she signed their CDs, posters, lanyards (and also the copies of the Double Vinyl records for the ones who had them). And I'm not forgetting Kevin. He got a chance to get his laminate signed and to take pictures with Jenny too. How amazing a night it was when we all helped each other by taking pictures and videos of each other when it was time to meet up close and personal with Jenny.

After all the Acers got their chance, I forgot about my posters, so I asked Jenny to sign them for me. She was so thankful, and I was happy too. We hugged each other at the end and took the final picture, just the two of us. Even though every meet & greet is different, I felt like this one was the best so far.

After the meet & greet, we all went outside to have something to eat and drink. Many of us went to a Five Guys restaurant where we spent time processing the great moment we had just experienced with Jenny.

Jessi, Kevin, and I got inside the venue early by using our All Access passes. We positioned ourselves right in front at the center of the stage. (We had the option to be inside the gate, but Jessi and I realized that the best option was to be outside the gate to be able to get as many pictures and as much film as we wanted. So we did it that way.) Just before the crowd got in, we made some space for the Acers who were waiting in line.

Once everyone got together, we were set to see Jenny on stage. But first, it was going to be Snap, then Jenny, and La Bouche with Tanya from Culture Beat. Of course, we were all cheering for Jenny. We enjoyed the show from start to finish, even though Jenny's voice was still struggling a bit with pneumonia.

After the show, Kevin, Jessi, and I remained inside the venue. Taking advantage of the All Access passes, we went backstage without any trouble. That was nice. So inside, we found Jenny again and we talked with her for a bit. We also saw Jakob, and he was bleeding a little bit. During the show, he hit his guitar against his forehead. We were like wow, but he was okay. (We told him, well, I guess this is part of the job, hehehe.)

When talking to Jenny backstage, I complimented her performance. Jessi asked how she was feeling because of her ongoing recovery from pneumonia. She was hanging in there, but boy, she still tried to give us her best. I thanked her for everything and we mentioned again that it was because of her that Kevin and I arranged our trip to Europe based on her London concert, and she just smiled. Then we ended up talking about the *My Story* vinyl. And she confessed that she actually didn't have a vinyl record player. I said, "What? You don't have a turntable, Jenny?" She said, "No, now I will have to buy one." Wow, she surprised me with that answer.

I also mentioned to her that one of my favorite songs is "Come" from the Swedish TV program she did a few years ago. I told her that I loved the moment when she got emotional as Lisa Nilsson performed her version of "The Sign" in Swedish. I told her, "I cried with you." That's when Kevin told Jenny, "I saw Roberto first watch that program on YouTube in Swedish with no subtitles and he got emotional without understanding a word of what was being said." (But then, I added that I watched the same episode with the English subtitles later). Jenny then told us why she got emotional. Jenny explained that during the filming of the TV program, Lisa told only Jenny that she was going through a painful divorce, so when Lisa was singing "The Sign," Jenny understood the meaning of that performance and her tears came from empathizing with Lisa's pain.

One more picture and it was time to say goodbye. Once again, we hugged each other, wished her the best, and thanked her for the great time we had. Outside the venue, Dave, David, Anja, and Wazzi were waiting for us. We decided to go for a drink to finish celebrating our amazing night. A couple of drinks later, and we were heading out of the O2 Arena.

The next morning, Kevin and I went to meet my Aunty (my father's sister) and cousin. I had not seen them for more than thirteen years. She was struggling with a strong cancer treatment too, so that's why I said that this trip to Europe was meaningful in many ways.

Later, we met with Jessi and Anja again who were waiting patiently for us in central London. Once we arrived, we waited for Wazzi too. He chose the place for dinner, a place with traditional British pies. And he picked well. We enjoyed one last meal together then took the final pictures. Dave nicknamed us "Londonbase" because we looked like a band (maybe due to the light effect, I don't know, but we did look like a band). That was our last moment together, at least with Anja and Jessi because Wazzi, Kevin, and I were planning to meet again in Paris a few days later. So we said goodbye temporarily to Wazzi. But Anja and Jessi were going back to Germany the next day.

We took the metro to our hotels. I remember Jessi and I were laughing so hard because our heads were reflecting in front of the window of the metro wagon in a funny way. Maybe a sign that we all had so much fun in the days we spent together. I also remember Anja's sad face she made at me when it was time for the last hug before getting off the metro train. I will always be thankful for their friendship. I've missed them!

The next days were busy with sightseeing: Windsor and Stonehenge, the rest of London, a *Mamma Mia* play, and dinner with my cousin and Aunty again. The days passed so quickly. The next weekend, I was already in Amsterdam visiting my friends from high school after a long absence. I kept filming videos dedicated to my father and sending them to him every other day. After Amsterdam, Kevin and I traveled to Brussels for about two days (beautiful city). But to put the perfect end to this trip, Paris awaited us, and Wazzi too. And what a great way to start in Paris. We met Wazzi again, as promised, and visited a nice French restaurant.

It was our first night in Paris and the last night for Wazzi. We all had tickets to the amazing and famous *Moulin Rouge* show. (The show was out of this world. I would say very French?) After the show, we had traditional crêpes!! Delicious! And sadly, it was time to say goodbye to Wazzi. The next day, he would travel to Germany where he was going to meet with Jessi again in Berlin. For Kevin and I, we still had five more days ahead of the Parisian beauties—including the Louvre Museum with the famous Mona Lisa, Notre Dame, the Eiffel Tower, and more French cuisine.

On May 6th, it was time to get back to the US. I was thankful for all the good moments during this trip: the quality time I spent with my extended family and high school friends, the opportunity to see Jenny (and to be more up close and personal with her), and for the great people I met for the first time and the bonds we made. What a great fellowship of Acers we've got. I hope I can see everyone again in the near future. (Maybe there could be another chance to see Jenny again and plan another European trip, including Germany. Why not?)

As I wrap up this story of my experiences over the last couple of years, all I have to say is that we have to still believe in dreams. Believe that dreams come true, sooner or later, as when I thought I would never meet my favorite band like Ace of Base. And in this case, my favorite band member, Jenny. Or dreams like meeting the love of your life. Sometimes dreams can come true. It might be cliché to say "Don't Stop Believin'," like the Journey song.

It all makes me think about my father again. I won't stop believing that he can recover and get better in the near future, despite being already four months in the hospital. I am hopeful for a brighter future.

Kevin, Roberto, and Jessi backstage after the London show (2018)

ABOUT THE AUTHOR: Roberto Chang was born in Lima, Peru and moved to the United States in 2006. He now lives in the US state of Virginia. Ace of Base has been part of his life since his youth in 1993 when the *Happy Nation* album started spinning on Peruvian radio. He immediately fell in love with their music and they have been the soundtrack of his life ever since—during the hard times, the struggles, and the many moments of happiness.

The Sign: A Personal Meaning

by Nikki

The first time I heard "The Sign" was in October 1994 at a Halloween carnival. As a nine-year-old girl, it was the beat of the music that caught my attention rather than the lyrics, of course. My love for, and loyalty to, Ace of Base started that Friday night. And now, I look back and realize that the words of "The Sign" did speak to me as a child, as they do today.

My life has been blessed with family and friends who love and support me. But growing up with a physical disability like cerebral palsy can often be a challenge. Still today, when I hear the words "life is demanding without understanding," I pause and think how people who are different, such as myself, are not always understood and accepted by others. I ask myself questions like, "Where do I belong in society?"

It's interesting that when I visited Sweden five years ago, the home country of Ace of Base, the Swedes saw me first and the wheelchair second. I was immediately treated as an equal. Yet in my own county, I'm often treated very differently.

Then there are other words in the song that, instead of putting me in a reflective mood, they just make me smile! Like "I got a new life, you would hardly recognize me," and "No one's gonna drag you up to get into the light where you belong." Those words make me appreciate the life I was given in a new home at age four. They also make me feel confident that I'm in charge of my own happiness. I have to put myself in the light where I belong and deserve to be! Ace of Base's music, especially "The Sign," always puts me in a good mood—especially when I am frustrated or when I'm feeling down. I'm so grateful for their music.

Nikki touring Stockholm by ferry near the amusement park (2013)

ABOUT THE AUTHOR: Nikki is a Southern girl, born and raised in the United States. She has been blessed to be part of a loving family and network of friends who have supported her and encouraged her to do the things she loves: enjoying music, exploring history, reading, traveling, and serving her community (volunteering at a local hospital and working with horses in a hippotherapy program). Thanks to being introduced to Ace of Base—the best music group ever—she has always enjoyed learning about Sweden and making lifelong friends from there. She had the opportunity of a lifetime in 2013 when she took an eleven-day trip to Sweden where she was able to see all the history she had been studying for years. She found Stockholm to be amazing, especially the Vasa, the Old Town, and the ABBA Museum.

Once Upon a Time in Poland

by Alan Kardyka

It all started in 1993. My older sister discovered a new band called Ace of Base. She was totally fascinated with them. Fascination with their first album, *Happy Nation,* was not only her thing—it was a time when everybody everywhere listened to Ace of Base. I remember when I was in school before my gymnastics lesson. I was waiting in the hall watching a group of girls taking a dance lesson; they were dancing to the "Happy Nation" song. Anyway, my sister asked our mother for a cassette of Ace of Base. Unfortunately, our mom bought a cassette called "Acce of Mega Basse"—it was a bootleg of course (and she hadn't know it).

After 1989, Poland entered into a new political and social system—we could finally buy luxury goods from the Western countries. What is more, everything was new for us so we were not fully prepared to adjust the law to the new requirements. As a consequence, there were no regulations in Poland about copyright from 1989 to 1994. This is why there were so many bootlegs and pirate copies of music in Poland. And it was one-hundred percent legal. Even when I and my sister tried to buy an original Ace of Base cassette in our small town, there were only bootlegs left because everybody had bought all the original stuff from the music stores.

Days passed, I grew up, and the band's music accompanied me during my adolescence. My sister focused on her teenage life and more mature music, and I was interested in Ace of Base more and more. I could finally buy my first original cassette from a friend from my class who wasn't fascinated with the band anymore. Unfortunately, when *The Bridge* came out, I couldn't find any copy of it in my entire town (even a bootleg). Finally, it all changed in the *Flowers* era. This was a memorable time for me for a few reasons. First, my friend bought the *Flowers* CD for my birthday. It was my first original CD album ever! My region at that time was very poor, so there were only cassettes in the music stores. After 1995, CDs slowly appeared, but albums were still much too expensive for most people (especially teenagers).

I was totally shocked about Linn's strange behavior when I saw the *Flowers* booklet. I was obsessed about it. "What is going on with her?" I even started to show to my friends the differences between her old and new role in the band. During a music lesson, everyone had to prepare a presentation about their favourite band. Of course, I prepared an Ace of Base story with the strange Linn history. Everybody was so interested, and I was proud that Linn was in the limelight.

There was also an opportunity to meet the band in my country; they played live at the Opole '98 Festival. However, I wasn't able to go there because I was too young and it was too far. Time passed, and their music still had an impact on me. I was in the last level before high school when *Singles Of The '90s* came out. Thanks to me, some of my friends decided to buy the album because I told them, "There are all smash hits on it!" To buy a CD of SOT90s, I had to take a trip to Warsaw because Ace of Base CDs were hard to find in music stores in smaller towns.

In Poland, it was an era when the internet appeared. Of course, the internet had come to my country in 1993, but for the public and most ordinary people, it became available in late 1998. Anyway, that era was a time when I started to discover the internet. It was the very first time I logged onto aceofbase.com (with a blue design in the style of SOT90s). It was also the very first time I chatted with people on the Ace of Base Paradise website. The first Acer I ever talked to was Jeff (Yes! I remember his name). I also discovered a website by Tino where I could listen to all the songs in RealPlayer format. I was shocked that there was a second version of "Life Is A Flower." I started to discover thousands of differences between the many versions of the US and European songs. (To this day, I still can't understand why they changed those few seconds on the US version of "Always Have, Always Will" instead of the perfect European ending? GOD, WHY!?)

I was in high school when Ace of Base turned into the big silence. Fortunately, their music was still with me. It helped me in many hard moments in my life because their songs always remind me of my good, innocent childhood. Then suddenly, *Da Capo* came out. I logged into the new forum on the official website. And I met Acers from the whole world on The Hallo Boards. When I was a teenager, high school was a difficult time for me so I started to search out alternative, good, and positive emotions on the boards. I found many Acers who became some kind of "virtual friends." So the virtual life of Acers was also important for me. Moreover, I could finally talk to other people who were as crazy as I about the band.

The most crazy thing I have done during that era was to create a way to buy *Da Capo: The DVD*. I couldn't buy it on Amazon because I had no credit card yet, and my parents were not ready to trust the internet or its safety. Because the DC DVD was released only in Germany and Sweden, I decided to do my best to get on the team of the best students of German in my high school because they were going on a trip to Germany. I qualified for the group so I could go with them on the unique school trip to Germany. I went only to buy the *Da Capo* DVD.

After arriving in Munster, we didn't have any free time. But then, our group had a task: our teachers wanted to check our language skills. Each of us had to go to a shop and find some special prizes of hard-to-find products. The prizes gave us a special code for the next task. During this task, I went into the Saturn store and searched the DVD shelf. And then…. I saw the sign—I mean, I saw the *Da Capo* DVD, and my heart beat so hard. I bought the DC DVD, spending almost all the money that my mom gave me for the trip (*Da Capo* cost about 25 euro, which is more than 100 złoty, so for a Polish guy, the German DVDs were four times more expensive).

The Redefined era was a time when I focused on my studies, so it wasn't an active time for me. The real thing happened when the dotty-girls era came out. I was totally disappointed: New girls. No Jenny. A statement from Ulf about Linn. I decided to do everything I could to make my dreams come true: meet Acers, meet Aces, and go to an Acer Meeting. I knew that I had to be fast because the time of the band was coming to an end. This is why I organized a Polish Acer meeting and then an International Acer Meeting (in Poznań). I decided to create the Ace of Base HOUSE website to rescue all the memories of the band from all the great websites that were closing down more and more. I also tried to resuscitate The AceBoards to keep Acers online there. Unfortunately, Facebook changed the way of the communities, so it was just a matter of time until I realized it wasn't worth an effort.

I have to also write about my first meeting with Jenny in 2013. A fan meeting was planned after her performance in the Velodrom in Berlin, so I went to Germany to meet her. This is how it started:

THE BEGINNING

First, there were thousand of plans and discussions about an IAM in Sweden with Jonas, or in Berlin for the European Acers. Unfortunately, it was always only speculations so nothing came of it. Suddenly, someone posted on The AceBoards and Facebook that Jenny was going to hold a show in Berlin. I thought it might be a reason for the organization of an Acer Meeting in Germany, so I started talking about it on TAB! Jessi and Anja took over the baton and immediately got down to work. It started as a European Acer Meeting, but there were Acers from outside Europe even, so it turned into the International Acer Meeting 2013! Thanks to Jessi and Anja, we all have the greatest memories, and now you can read the details of this special day (and night).

PREPARING FOR DEPARTURE

I'm sitting and trying to purchase a ticket for the 90s Mega Sause where Jenny will sing live, but there are some technical problems. Fortunately, it all goes OK. Suddenly, Pablo rings. I hang up my mobile phone and it looks like he wants to go there with me. I ring to my friend Barthezz—he will go also, but on his own. We all are so excited. The guest list on the Facebook profile grows more and more. Jessi writes that she needs to know who will be there... I thought that she must be organising some big surprise, otherwise she wouldn't ask. Days go by and finally the 23rd of November has come!

"What a beautiful morning," I thought, and realised I was a little bit late. Shit! Pablo and my friend, who is also going with us, are gonna be here in a moment! I'm taking the fastest shower in my life and making a second breakfast for the ride. I'm running to the tram. I hope I will not be late to pick up Pablo and my friend from the station. Gosh! I forgot my tickets for the Berlin show at home... I will come back after meeting with the guys. Pablo wants a coffee. We are sitting in some restaurant, but time is running out. We have to go!

All three of us go to the bus station where we have a departure to Berlin. Unfortunately, I have to go back for our tickets. Meanwhile, Pablo and my friend lose the way to the bus station. We have only ten minutes left. I decide that I will go to the station on my own and ask the chauffeur to wait for them. Fortunately, everybody gets in at the right time and the right place.

We are sitting on the bus and going to Berlin. One hour later, another drama: there is an unexpected personal control at the border. One of the passengers has some trouble and our bus is standing still. We have an hour delay. Pablo says, "We're not gonna make it. We will be late for the meeting with the other Acers!" (Jessi wrote that the meeting is at 7:00 p.m.) Suddenly, our bus moves!

We are in Berlin, searching for the S-Bahn (German trams.. nice communication by the way). It is 6:30 p.m. and we've lost the way to our hotel since none of us have internet and can't get to our GPS navigation. Yes, here it is. We finally found it! We go to the room, and suddenly Jessi makes a phone call to me. She asks, "Alan, where are you?! If you want to see Jenny, come quickly." None of us know that Jessi has changed the time of the meeting because the internet is not free in the German hotels, so none of us have internet where Jessi has sent the message. Our friend is in the toilet… Me and Pablo can't wait one minute longer, so we run to the Velodrom, which is just next to our hotel.

Finally, we see some groups standing in front of the entrance gate. I recognize Lily from The AceBoards and Michael too. I say, "Pablo! Look, it's Lily. It must be the Acers!" They are waiting for something or someone. We shake hands to say hallo and I ring Jessi. She answers, "Do you see the security man over there? I'm there." I walk over to see where Jessi is, and suddenly, I recognize her inside the Velodrom. But a security guard stops me. I call the other Acers over. They come over and we wait to see what happens next. Then Jessi comes out from behind the gate and says to the security guard that we are the guests. He lets us in. Excitement and tension grows...

UNEXPECTED CONFERENCE

Jessi leads us through a long hall. Nobody knows what will happen. Suddenly, we enter into some room. Looks like a conference room: modest refreshments are set around the tables and chairs. In the middle, there is a special place with t-shirts and CDs. Anja is waiting for us inside. We all take a seat in suspense, wondering what will happen next. Deep silence falls. I decide to take control for a moment to relieve the tension. I say, "Introduce yourselves to everyone, tell us your nickname, and where you come from." Successively, we present ourselves, and then suddenly, something is happening. I'm sitting with my back turned away from the entrance, but I see a great stir on the faces of the other Acers. I'm thinking, "No way, it must be her," and there she is: Jenny!

She enters the room quietly, modestly saying "Hi." She is surrounded by bodyguards, two singers, and a guy in a red shirt. "Come closer," she says, "What do you want to do now? Maybe let's start with the autographs?" Everybody moves to her with their CDs and cameras. I'm the last one in the queue, but suddenly more Acers appear. They are late but happy that they can meet Jenny too. Everybody gets a short chat with Jenny. First, Jenny gives an autograph and then speaks to each Acer. I'm touched when she talks with Lily. It's amazing that Jenny remembers her fans and she is so sensitive.

Now, my turn! The words are confusing me; the impression is too big. Jenny is looking at me. I see her dark, big eyes with black eyeliner. I love her hair and she looks so fine. I'm thinking: "Wow, no picture can show other Acers how good and young she looks." I say to her that my choir wants to send her some cheers and I won't be able to sing with them on Saturday because I'm here at her performance. I ask, "Can I touch you Jenny?" And spontaneously, I'm kissing her hand while posing for pictures. (God! I kissed her hand!)

After all the autographs, it's time for a photo shoot. Jenny gets up from the table and goes under an archway where Acers take pictures of her with her two singers. Now, it is time for pictures with the fans. Everybody comes up to take a few pictures with her. Jenny is very patient and poses from all sides. Everywhere, flickering flashes of cameras over and over. This moment lasts forever. Jenny has almost angelic patience: we are taking pictures more and more. And finally, we sit down to hear what Jenny has to say.

THE INTERVIEW

Jenny is open to answering all questions. Now is the time for us to ask, so I ask her three questions: "Jenny, do you still sing in the church? I ask because we considered inviting you to our church in Poland, but I'm not sure if you have considered visiting Poland?" She answers that indeed she still sings in churches and she likes to hold performances in Europe, so Poland would be great. I also ask her about this famous promotional video from YouTube where we can hear "Give Me The Faith" in a lower key: "Does this version exist, or it is just a short part for the promotional video?" She answers that there are more than a hundred versions of this song. And my last question is about a reunion, "Jenny.. I'm not sure it is polite to ask you about here, but just answer YES or NO." (And suddenly she is laughing saying, "NO, noooo!") I continue my question, "Do you want to come back to Ace of Base?" She answers that she is always open for a reunion. There are many more question from other Acers, but I'm too excited to remember them all. She talks about her future plans and about her demos, which leaked to the internet (and because of that she cannot use them for her next project). She also says that she will perform one song from *My Story*. At the end, Jenny says that she remembers us in her prayers. She also asks us for support during her concert. After the meeting, I go with Pablo to the hotel to rest because Jenny's show will be late, at 2:30 a.m. In the hotel, my friend is waiting for us. After a small break, we decide to take a walk before the show.

VELODROM SPLENDOUR

We go to eat something but can't find the right restaurant. Suddenly, Pablo yells: "Look! It's Jenny, sitting in the restaurant with three other people." I thought: "Naaah… He is joking." But it is her! We wave our hands at her and she smiles. We decide to respect her privacy and we don't go in and don't take pictures. We see that there are many people trying to get into the Velodrom, so we decide not to eat.

We're standing in a long queue into the Velodrom. Security is scrupulous. Finally, we enter the arena, and near the locker-room, a group of Acers are standing waiting for the rest of us. We all gather in front of the stage and, through these six hours, wait for Jenny's show. We dance all night together and I'm starting to feel a little tired. Unfortunately, the concert of Jenny is scheduled late. I conclude that the concert of Jenny is too late because people are already too drunk. Finally, at the end of the DJs' performance, they start to set microphones for Jenny, but they have some technical problems so the DJs keep playing. When I hear another *weiter*, I'm starting to get irritated. Finally, the DJs finish—and the announcement of Jenny appears on the big screen.

DYING TO STAY ALIVE

I`m so happy that I could die! Die to stay alive. There is a black screen. And suddenly, Jenny appears on the screen like on the promotional video. She is talking about untold stories. We hear the "Intro" with the "Kyrie" from *My Story*, and on the screen I see a church stained-glass window. Suddenly, I see war and a big nuke and many pictures. Jenny walks onto the stage with her singers performing "Happy Nation" with choreography similar to the Redefined tour. Her voice is so clear and good. Now I'm thinking, "God! No way… I thought it would be like on YouTube. Is this how it works? At the concert, it sounds good, but when you record it, the sound effects are worse." Now, she performs "Wheel of Fortune." It is a new version similar to the 2008 version, but better. And I told Pablo, "You will see that she will perform 'Dying to Stay Alive'." And I'm right! She is performing "Dying to Stay Alive" LIVE! She is perfect in it. I am in such a big impression.

Next songs are: "Lucky Love," "All That She Wants," "Life Is A Flower," "Cruel Summer," and "Beautiful Life." The worst arrangement is LIAF—it is a song that nobody can change. It doesn't work. And LIAF was horrible. It is the only song where I'm thinking, "WTF is that!?" I think Acers like it, but people want to hear the music of the '90s (because it is a party of the '90s), not the new versions, and the LIAF arrangement is totally shit here. My favourite arrangement so far is "Happy Nation." It is modern and sounds awesome!

Jenny sings so sensational that the time is passing very quickly. Suddenly, she leaves the stage. Fortunately, she is back with the big song: "The Sign." Right after her performance, I tell my friend that I want to go back to the hotel because I'm dying… dying because I am tired and I want to stay alive, not dying. We go back to the hotel, but unfortunately, there is such a big queue at the toilet! Drama!

NEVER ENDING STORY

After returning home, I receive new Facebook invitations and messages. Everybody is uploading pictures from the show. Facebook's notifications are growing by the hour. My mailbox fills up and heats up to red! I'm back at home with 250 notifications. It is a never ending story till now. I'm sitting here writing this article and thinking about the people who I've met in Berlin. Thank you all. You are in my heart. It is nice to be an Acer—and now Lily's husband Danny, who was there with her, knows how it is to be an Acer. Stay united! Stay Ace!

I hope you had fun reading my story of the band's impact on my life. I described each era, the most interesting phases of it in my life, and the meeting with Jenny in Germany. Those memories are still living in me. I will keep them forever.

Alan's creativity is showcased on his YouTube channels

ABOUT THE AUTHOR: Alan lives in Poland and has been an Acer since the start. He is a teacher and musician with a PhD in theology. Creativity describes him best, which you can see on his YouTube channels: Czercz Czanel and Diligent Natan. Alan conducts training sessions on working with youth, threats, and dangers in cyberspace. He has also published three scientific monographs.

Memories Forever

by Linda Stuiver

The members of Ace of Base, and especially Jenny, have given me so many amazing memories. I can honestly say my life would not have been the same without them. For me, it all started in 1994 when I bought my first ever CD, *Happy Nation*. I didn't even have a CD player back then. I started collecting articles, CDs, singles, and everything else I could find about the band. To get more articles from around the world, I started writing to people from abroad. It was an amazing way to get to know other Acers, some of whom I still talk to now, over twenty years later!

Jenny has always been my favourite member of the band. There is just something so special about her! Of course, I love her voice, but most of all she comes across as such a warm, caring, and sweet person. I have met her a few times now, and I can say that my first impression about her was so right! She is one-hundred percent the person I expected and hoped her to be. Another reason why I love her so much is her strong faith and the big heart she has. She truly has an incredible personality. And a great sense of humor, too.

Back in the early nineties, I was struggling with my sexuality. I didn't know if I would ever fall in love with a boy, or if it was only girls I liked. I had no clue how to tell friends or family. When I was thirteen, I finally knew I was gay. I didn't feel any attraction towards boys at all. And also, I convinced myself I was actually "in love" with Jenny. Looking back now, I think it was safer for me to "fall in love" with someone that I would never even meet (or so I thought). And I finally found the strength to tell my parents in a letter. They were, and still are, so supportive of me. What also helped me a lot is that Jenny is also a Christian like me, and she never seemed to have any problems with other people being gay. This made me feel better about myself.

In 1998, I met the four members of Ace of Base for the first time. I didn't think that day would ever come… It was surreal. Jonas, Ulf, and Linn were all in the VIP restaurant where a security man took me after he saw me waiting outside for hours. I got to chat and take pictures with them. It was amazing. But I couldn't help but ask myself where Jenny was. Eventually I dared to ask, and it turned out she was still in her dressing room getting ready for the show. "Well, too bad, that's it," I said to myself. But Ulf came to the rescue. He took me upstairs to the dressing room! Jenny still had curlers in her hair, but we got to talk for a few minutes and she signed some things for me. That night, I went home knowing my dream had come true! An experience that I would never forget.

The next day, they were still in the Netherlands and I went again. Jenny recognized me and we took the picture that we didn't get to take the day before.

During my teenage years, I developed some pretty serious mental health issues. But the music from Ace of Base was always there to cheer me up. It really helped me through some dark times in my life. Whenever I felt down, I played songs like "Beautiful Life" and "Life Is A Flower" really loud. Sometimes I would cry and scream, but the songs helped to get my emotions out. Something I never knew how to do back then.

Another song that has always been very special to me is Jenny's "Give Me The Faith." This is, and will always be, the most precious song to me. I could really relate to it; it has such a powerful message. And it also helped me to really keep my faith when things seemed hopeless. Sometimes I wondered if I was even worthy of God's love, destroying my body like I did. That's when I loved listening to Jenny's more religious songs. They helped me understand that we are all God's children and that He will forever love me.

After seeing Ace of Base a few times at Night of the Proms in Belgium in 2005, I saw them again in 2007 at a Copenhagen concert. This one was incredibly special. I got to meet so many Acers from around the world. Also, it was just a few weeks after my first inpatient treatment for anorexia. I really needed something to cheer me up, to let me see that life was worth living. And that is exactly what that weekend in Copenhagen did! Being surrounded by fellow Acers, having so much fun together, and the amazing concert and meeting… That was all I needed!

Copenhagen was amazing, but I was still struggling a lot and I couldn't really find my way. I didn't know how to love myself. So for years, I continued going from one treatment centre to another. When Jenny's album, *My Story*, was released, I took it with me everywhere I went. "Give Me The Faith" was still my special song. I shared it with other patients during music therapy, to hopefully let them feel what I felt when I listened to it. Most of them had no clue who this Jenny Berggren was, but they could really FEEL the song.

Finally, in 2015, Jenny came to the Netherlands again. On that day in December, I celebrated my thirty-fourth birthday with some close friends. But all I could think about was that Jenny was in my country. So, the birthday party ended early so me and a friend could drive to the north of the Netherlands for the show. My friends were totally okay with it, as they knew how much this meant to me. This was the most special day of my life. I still have the roses that Jenny threw at me during the show.

After the incredible show, me and my friend waited outside to hopefully meet Jenny. It was a cold December night, but I didn't dare go to the car to get a coat, afraid I would miss Jenny. So we waited for hours, not even sure if Jenny was still inside. My friend tried to convince me to leave a few times, but I refused. I would have stayed all night. And finally, we saw Jenny's car leaving the gate, driving past. I was devastated. I thought that was it.

But the car stopped! Jenny and her backing singers came out. I got a huge hug from Jenny. She was so sweet, she offered us drinks and some food, and even her coat to wear because I was freezing. She saw the scars on my arms, and gave me another big hug and spoke some really encouraging words. This meeting really showed how much of a caring person she is. She told me to keep the coat until I was warm and send it back to her later. I will never forget this day. It was amazing when, a few days later, she shared a picture of her and me on her Instagram, saying I have a special place in her heart. So do you Jenny, so do you!

In 2016, a friend and I drove to Belgium to see Jenny again. But due to heavy traffic and bad weather, we didn't make it in time. We waited for hours backstage, only to find out she had already left.

But in 2017, I got another chance, so I went to Oberhausen, Germany all by myself. Having an anxiety disorder, this was a pretty big deal, but I made it. And again, I had a really good time! Meeting up with old and new Acers was so much fun. And, of course, seeing Jenny live again and meeting her. She even remembered me. I had a great weekend, and I knew this was not going to be the last time.

So here I am, writing this story, knowing that I will see Jenny, and a lot of Acers from around the world again, in Bonn, Germany. Just a few more months to go. I can't wait, it is going to be awesome, I just know it!

I want to say thank you to all Ace of Base and Jenny fans and friends for being the most amazing group of fans any artist can have. I love each and every one of you. And thank you to Jenny, for just being the incredible person you are. You changed my life for the better. I will forever love and support you!

Linda on her thirty-fourth birthday meeting Jenny (2015)

ABOUT THE AUTHOR: Linda Stuiver, a.k.a. Linn, was born in the city of s-Hertogenbosch in the Netherlands. She studied international media and entertainment management, and is currently doing volunteer work at a facility for people who suffer from dementia. She loves working with people, especially the elderly. Her hobbies include writing, attending concerts, crafting, drafting letters, cuddling with her two guinea pigs named Lion and Tatum, and spending time with family and friends, especially her sweet four-year-old nephew.

Dreams Come True

by Farkhod Yadgarov

It was the beginning of a new era full of hope and uncertainty at the same time. The country where I was born disappeared a few years before 1993. I was fourteen years old back then. In the beginning of the independence of Uzbekistan, I was excited about new horizons and opportunities, but the reality was more cruel.

To survive, we had a small farm at our house. I had to wake up at 5:00 a.m. to feed dozens of cows, bulls, sheep, hundreds of chickens and rabbits while also working to be a good student with good grades. Everything I believed in also disappeared with the Soviet Union. I didn't know how it would transform my life. I was a teenager who was lost.

One day, everything made sense again—through music. I heard a beat, a beat that was not common, that was different from the others. I didn't even know who was singing. I stopped next to our old television and tried to remember some words of the song, even if I didn't speak a word of English. It was "All That She Wants." I was singing it wrong, but the song stuck in my head. At the end of the video, I saw the name of the band: Ace of Base. I repeated it again and again to not forget.

After a while, my brother brought a cassette tape and put it in a player. And I heard that beat. It was another song, but I recognized them. The songs were playing one after another, there was ATSW too. I was so happy and didn't stop singing "O machi bos" or something like that during ATSW.

I loved the whole album and I had some favorite songs on it. I didn't understand what the band was singing about and truly wanted to know. I decided to learn English. And each time when I was listening to Ace of Base, I tried to translate their songs into my own language.

I didn't know anything about the band, not their names, not where they were from. Only after several years, I knew that they were Jenny, Linn, Jonas, and Ulf. I learned to recognize the voices of the two sisters and I became a Jennier (fan of Jenny). I found the voice of Jenny to be sharper, higher, and more defined—and I never understood why her vocals were featured less on the first album than Linn's. I thought it was a bit unfair. So I was happy about the contribution of Jenny in the next albums.

Since my childhood, I wanted to travel, but it was quite impossible for many reasons. One of those reasons was my level of English. The songs of Ace of Base helped me to learn it, and thanks to it, I could find a job abroad.

Very early, when I worked on the farm, I understood that I wanted to change my life and the only way to do so was to leave my home country and take a chance abroad. My first destination was Dubai. I discovered a world of luxury retail, and it still fascinates me. My first job was in a five-star hotel. After that was a luxury department store. Then I moved to France where I continued to work for the biggest luxury groups, such as LVMH and Richemont. Now, I hold two MBA diplomas: French (ESSEC) and German (Mannheim). Here, I have to say that my willingness to learn English when I discovered the music of Ace of Base played a huge role because all the courses were in English.

My dream came true. Now I live in Europe. It is where I first understood the real meaning of freedom. I can travel and express myself freely without any fear, which is not common in my country. I travel, I've learned other languages, I meet new, great people each day (like other Acers and fans of Jenny). It is a great community where we share our great moments, passions, and memories.

It was in Almaty in Kazakhstan when I saw Ace of Base for the first time on stage. Winter, February 2007. It was cold and snowy. I travelled thousands of kilometers, crossed three countries to finally be able to see them live. I travelled in a bus and there was a snowstorm on the way. The driver wanted to stop the bus, and I was thinking only about the concert and reaching it on time.

The concert was great! Jenny, Jonas, and Ulf were on stage. They sang a new version of "The Sign," "Beautiful Life," "All That She Wants," "Life Is A Flower," etc. It lasted one hour and fifteen minutes, but it was enough for me to feel happy and satisfied. People were singing and dancing, even if the venue was not made for it (there were seats). I had goosebumps. But I didn't have a chance to meet them. I couldn't even imagine meeting one of the band members one day.

It was another winter's day when I visited a small church in Sweden. A guy called Dmitriy, an Acer from Russia, told me that Jenny was going to speak at a conference in Jönköping. It didn't take long to decide. We met in Stockholm, and from there, we took a train to Jönköping.

Dmitriy and I stepped into the church, and I saw her. I lost all the words I had prepared in my head before arriving there. She walked up to us and said, "Hello, I'm Jenny." I could only reply, "Yes, I know." She continued with a smile, "And you?" "I'm Farkhod from Uzbekistan."

She invited us to join the people who were already waiting for her speech and said that we could meet her after. It seemed so unreal to me. She asked us to introduce ourselves to the people who were sitting in the room. She said that we had travelled all the way to see her there that night. It made me feel like a special guest. I said that I was from Uzbekistan. Nobody even knew where it was. I offered a traditional silk scarf from my country to Jenny, which she wore during her speech. The conference was in Swedish. I didn't understand any word of it, but it didn't matter.

After her speech, we had a talk with her and she invited us to Gothenburg for another conference. We went there and she sang "Ravine." It was divine. It was the only song she sang that night. I wished she had never stopped. The atmosphere of a church gave another dimension to what I was living that night.

The conferences took place during the decision to take two new girls into the band. We talked about the decision, of course. Dmitriy and I said that we disagreed with it, and most fans did also. Jenny somehow tried to convince us that she would continue singing and she gave us the chance to listen to "Here I Am" from her new upcoming solo album. I loved it, and for me, it was the first real song of Ace of Base after so many years, after *Da Capo*. That evening, she told me I had eyes like her father. It was so emotional because she was very close to her father.

I bought a digital copy of *My Story* the first hour after its release. I was so impatient and exited. And the physical CD I got later during another meeting with Jenny. I found the solo album to be more mature than any of the albums by Ace of Base. It's like we grew up and the music of Jenny grew up with us. It's closer to me, to Farkhod-adult; mature and experienced.

The songs helped me overcome some circumstances in my life. My favorite song was "Numb," and it is still the one. It has a strong connection with some personal moments. "Gotta Go" also. It's like telling my own story—sometimes we have to leave and just go. I listen to the album still today and enjoy it as much as the first day.

Jenny is an amazing person with a big heart. Her personality, her involvement in charity, and her willingness to share always inspires me. For example, Jenny's work as an ambassador for the Voi Project (a project supported by the Swedish Church that helps African orphans). She always remembers all her fans by their names. She is very attentive and takes time with each of us.

Each meeting with her, organised by Jessi and Anja, marks a part of the greatest moments in my life. Those meetings remind me of my roots, from where I started, and that there are other people like me: Acers, Jenniers who get inspiration from Jenny to move forward, to reach their goals despite everything.

Farkhod in Gothenburg before the second conference (2010)

ABOUT THE AUTHOR: Farkhod was born in Bukhara, an ancient city more than two thousand years old in Uzbekistan. He now lives permanently in Europe, in France. He is passionate about history, travel, urban structure, urban planning, city architecture, and sites developed by man—as well as the beauty of natural sites such as beaches, volcanoes, and other wonders of nature. His interests are focused on both contemporary and industrial architecture of the last century. Farkhod also loves music, especially the music of the '90s.

Life is So Precious in Your Hands

by Ric Rijnders

On the beach, there was a Christmas tree. And I spent my time on the beach in its shadow. My family and I heard a lot of Ace of Base both on the beach and in the resort that Christmas. One of the bartenders must have been a fan because he played the entire *Happy Nation* album several times a day. I was so influenced by it, that soon enough I also loved the music and could sing along to every song. However, I had no idea who the artist was and it didn't occur to me to ask or find out.

After we returned home to the Netherlands from our Gran Canaria vacation, I happened to hear one of the songs on the radio. Luckily, the radio DJ said the artist's name and I immediately wrote it down. I went to the store and asked the shop owner if he knew this band and had any of their CDs. He brought me the album and let me listen to it to see if this was the music I was talking about. With every song I heard, my enthusiasm grew. I recognized almost all of them. Wonderful! I just *had* to get the album. And another Acer was born.

"Beautiful Life": the title and lyrics of a song that has changed lives. I don't know if Jonas ever figured it would change lives when he wrote this hit song, but it did.

The Bridge, the album with the song "Beautiful Life," was released when I was seventeen years old. It is a wonderful album (my favourite) with not just fun, upbeat songs but also sensitive, personal songs like "Ravine."

Several months later, I came out of the closet. And as an eighteen-year-old teenager, I went out to discover the world. Unfortunately, I also discovered the dark side of the world. I was sexually abused with a knife to my throat. As you can imagine, that event had a huge impact on my life. I started feeling deeply depressed and didn't dare go out into the world anymore.

At some point, I reached a very dark place in myself and I wanted to end my life. I had gathered a bunch of pills and was sitting on the edge of my bed with those pills in my hand. I didn't know if this would be the right decision because it would hurt my sweet parents greatly and leave them heartbroken. But I also didn't know how to go on with life like this.

Still holding the pills, I put on a CD. I wanted to hear my favourite band one more time. The music started, and for the first time, I didn't just hear the lyrics, I listened to the words—and they hit me: "It's a beautiful life! Take a walk in the park when you feel down, there are so many things there that's gonna lift you up, see the nature in bloom, a laughing child…"

Wow! That hit me hard. But not just that, those words also planted strength and hope in my heart. Of course, I would never have been able to write this if I had gone through with my attempt. And I am glad the entire band have had such an influence on me. I am immensely grateful for that.

Fortunately, heavy memories aren't the only memories or connections I have with the band. Ace of Base is also the base for a strong, ongoing friendship. In 2003, I met a girl named Daisy van Vugt who is a few years younger than me but who is also a fan. After corresponding back and forth, we decided to meet and get to know each other in real life. We hit it off, and after all these years, she is still one of my best friends. I am immensely grateful for that. I cherish her and our friendship and I hope we can enjoy it for many more years. We have gone through a lot together over the years, and although Ace of Base is not the main component of our friendship anymore, we still talk about them a lot. And they keep coming back, such as an Ace of Base-related present one of us gives the other—or mentioning this fan event in which fans write down their story.

In October 2005, I finally got the chance to see my musical heroes in real life and hear them play (at least three of the four, because Malin had stopped performing). But not just that, I also got the chance to meet them backstage at a fan meet & greet. Wow! What an overwhelming experience. I was jumping like a child; I didn't know how to contain my excitement. Fortunately, I was there with Daisy, so I could share it all with her.

I don't remember some of the questions and answers (because I was so nervous, haha). I do remember the hug I got from Jenny. During the signing session, we were all in line to have our items signed. We started with Jenny and then went on to Ulf and finally Jonas. Jenny had already signed my items, but I couldn't move on to Ulf and Jonas because they were still signing items and answering questions for other fans. This gave me an opportunity to give the fan letter that I had written at home to Jenny. It explained why they and the song "Beautiful Life" mean so much to me. I don't remember if she had already (partially) read the letter on the spot or if I just told her briefly what was in it, but my story moved Jenny deeply.

I got the idea that she didn't really know what to do because I was in line and there were other fans waiting behind me. I asked if I could give her a hug to thank her. Jenny tactfully told me I might get the chance to do that after the signing. This way, there wouldn't be any problems with the organization and with other fans doing the same during the signing. I understood and accepted it was probably too much to ask. However, the hold-up in front of me took so long, I couldn't move on to Ulf, so I had to stay in front of Jenny's table. Eventually Jenny stood up, bent over the table, and said something like, "What the heck, let's just do it." And I got my hug after all.

What a privileged moment that was for me. Not just because I got a hug from my idol, but because it symbolized the acknowledgement of my story and her involvement in it. As a fan, this meant the world to me. It contributed to my healing and how I have evolved as a person. Fortunately, photos were made of that moment and I sometimes look at them again full of admiration and pride.

Later, I pursued a degree in creative therapy. Part of the degree was learning to paint and deal with emotions. In my paintings, I sometimes used parts of lyrics (like "Love for Sale" when I did an internship in a clinic for addicts) or turned lyrics into pictures ("Ravine"). I haven't painted much since I've finished my degree, but I was once inspired by the video of "Here I Am" off Jenny's solo album (*My Story*). As you can see, my life has been constantly influenced by the band members and their music throughout the years.

Every once in a while, the Dutch radio station Qmusic plays the top 500 of the '90s. Listeners can vote for their own top twenty, which are then used to assemble the top 500. Of course, I voted for Ace of Base. You could also add a reason for voting for a particular song. I wrote that whenever I listen to Ace of Base, I always remember lying on the beach in the shade of a Christmas tree.

Because I wrote this, the radio channel called me on March 8th, 2018, and interviewed me briefly. The conversation would be aired approximately twenty minutes later. So right after we hung up, I called Daisy and she fortunately recorded it for me. Because of this story, she told me about the book project and that's how it all came full circle.

On March 9th, one day after my euphoric "fifteen seconds of fame" with Qmusic, my current partner Leon (my "Angel Eyes") and I got horrible news. He was diagnosed with lung cancer, which has spread to his lymph nodes. The doctors have unfortunately given him only a thirty percent chance of survival.

As I am writing this, my love is going through both chemotherapy and radiation therapy. He is fighting for his life. It is all very heavy and emotional and I am crying as I am writing. During these troubling events, I still try to get strength from Ace of Base's songs (though it is very difficult at this moment). The lyrics of songs like "I Pray," "Would You Believe," and "Beautiful Life" have a new meaning for me once again.

Because of this situation, we have also been forced to change our outlook on life and to set priorities. We will have to talk about difficult topics. However, we also try to focus on the positive things in our lives. If there is one thing we have learnt now, it is that time is precious. You have to get out of it what you can and enjoy it while you can. Therefore (and for legal reasons), we have decided to get married very soon. We don't know yet when or what it will be like, but our gut feeling tells us we should. Besides our parents and my friend Daisy, no one knows yet.

On Saturday, August 25th this year, Jenny will perform at the "We Love the 90's" party in Nijmegen. We had already bought the tickets before we knew Leon was ill. There's a big chance Jenny will sing "Beautiful Life" there as well. It has always been my favourite song, but I know it will be even more emotional than ever before because two days later on August 27th, Leon will undergo a scan. And just a few days after that, we will find out if his treatments have been successful or not. Of course, we hope and pray we are part of those thirty percent—and that on our wedding day, we can play "Beautiful Life" with an extra positive meaning. I pray…

I would like to thank The Jenny Source for giving me the chance to participate and to support charity. And most of all, I want to thank the band Ace of Base as a whole for everything. All the band members have equally contributed to my life. If it wasn't for them, my world would be completely different.

Despite my intense story, I want to convey to the readers the positivity in many of Jenny's and Ace of Base's songs. Listen to the lyrics and enjoy the melodies, which is why I will finish up with a quote:

> *"Life is a flower, so precious in your hands, carry on smiling and the world will smile with you."*

Jenny acknowledging Ric's story with a hug at a NOTP meet & greet
(2005)

ABOUT THE AUTHOR: Ric Rijnders was born in 1978 and grew up in a small town near Amsterdam called Monnickendam. Besides his love for Ace of Base, he loves his parents and Leon—his love and life mate—very much. (And a comic book series called ElfQuest too.) He currently works as a data manager in a high school and lives in The Hague in the Netherlands. In his spare time, he likes to draw, read, and take nice outdoor walks.

Let Music Take the Lead

by Rodrigo Navarrete Boettcher

My sister is the one who brought me into the Ace of Base world. She had the *The Sign* cassette in '93. I was around three years old, but I remember quite vividly "Dancer In A Daydream" playing in the background. I had this image in my mind that there was a blonde girl. I didn't even know there was a blonde girl, with leather jackets and all black and white. That's the image I had in my mind and it still pops up from time to time!

Thanks to them, I got to know Swedish pop, which is one of my favorite genres. The different rhythms and different styles from the band show the diversity they have in their songwriting and their production style. So their input has been fundamental in the way I consume music.

Jenny and Ace of Base have also influenced the way I see the creative side of my life. I am a graphic designer and I work building things, and their music has helped me explore creativity and thinking in a creative way.

I have a hobby that, in a big part, is thanks to Ace of Base and Jenny's work: music production. I have collaborated with various people around the globe, including Claes Cornelius from Mega Records, who I visited recently in Denmark, and Mike Ross from the United States, who is a great producer and DJ.

In 2015, I pitched Mike the idea of a remix project to be presented to Playground Music, the band's label, and we have done some tracks already from "The Bridge," which I hope get to see the light of day soon. Apart from this, I also make my own music and have invested in equipment over the years as a self-taught musician.

Evidently, the music from the guys and the girls has been a pretty big influence. It has made me take a career path in creative design and music production. All I have to say is big thanks to the band and Jenny. Because of them, I have built my creative side—both in my career and in my personal life—met wonderful Acers, and shared the passion of music with others.

Rodrigo visiting San Francisco, California, USA in 2017

ABOUT THE AUTHOR: Rodrigo Navarrete is from Santiago, Chile. He works as a graphic designer building web applications and brand identity, both in a firm and as a freelancer. His favorite Ace of Base song is "Never Gonna Say I'm Sorry," both musically and lyrically. His favorite Jenny song is "Beat Of My Heart." He runs the Ace of Base Hub website where he publishes demo versions and rarities of the band with the help of Claes Cornelius and other Ace of Base collaborators. You can reach Rodrigo on Facebook: facebook.com/rodrigo.navarrete.b

Growing Up with Ace of Base

by Elio Carrillo

It's funny how someone can be able to love and care about other people without ever having a chat, meeting him/her in person, talking to each other, and getting to know who they really are. That happens a lot between celebrities and their fans. And I must say, I am no exception when it comes to Ace of Base and my favorite singer ever: Jenny Berggren.

Anyways, I think my case is special. This feeling doesn't come from anything superficial. I'm not in love with their beauty, their looks, or the way they dress. I love them because of all the happiness they have brought to my life in many ways. When I think about how my life would have been without their influence, and without knowing all the amazing people I have met just because we share the same feelings for these musicians, I cannot feel anything less than blessed. I have a deep love and everlasting thankfulness to them.

My story starts in my home country Venezuela when I was only eight or nine years old. My two older brothers and my sister used to play songs from the *Happy Nation* album and the CD single of "The Sign" that they rented from a video club. I liked the band's music instantly. Ace of Base songs are some of the few tunes I can remember from my early childhood. When *The Sign: The Home Video* was released, my siblings rented the VHS tape from the video club too. I used to ask them to play it over and over. It was so cool. My native language is Spanish, so I wondered what the band members were saying. That curiosity woke in me an early interest in learning English.

In 1994 and 1995, their music was everywhere you go. "All That She Wants" was a must play at every party and "The Sign" and "Don't Turn Around" were played frequently on radio stations and TV. Ace of Base-fever cooled down in my country after 1996, with "Beautiful Life" being their last big hit. They weren't on TV or the radio so often anymore. They suddenly disappeared until 1998. That year, I remember my brothers and I were talking about Ace of Base, wondering what could have happened. We didn't have a clue as we didn't have access to the internet at that time.

Just about a week after that conversation, I was watching CNN News and I was shockingly surprised with the announcement of the band's new single and album, *Cruel Summer*! I was so excited, I ran to my brothers saying "Look, Ace of Base is back! What a coincidence. We were talking about them a few days ago." My brothers watched but their reaction was like "Ok, meh." But to me, it was totally different! I loved *Cruel Summer*!

I spent days watching music video channels to see if I could catch the video on tape. I even memorized the order that a lot of the videos were played in so I could predict when "Cruel Summer" would be broadcast. I wanted to record every second of the video from start to end. I think I got it on tape like ten times! I asked for the *Cruel Summer* album for Christmas and I got it. I was so happy with it.

Burned CDs were becoming popular. The video club that rented their CDs to us started selling everything because illegal copies were so cheap that no one was renting anymore. My brother got me the

229

Happy Nation album as a gift and I was so happy with it. When he told me they were selling all their stuff, I ran to the store and bought *The Sign: The Home Video*, but sadly the CD single was sold already.

I found myself playing the same tape over and over again, just as I did in my early childhood. But I knew other videos were missing, and I wanted to watch them again so much. It wasn't as easy as it is nowadays. One of my brothers used to record basketball and soccer games on tape. He told me he had recorded other Ace of Base videos on some of those tapes but he didn't know which ones. I checked all of his tapes for hours (he had about twenty) to find only one video, "Lucky Love." I was so happy anyway. I had to save it so it didn't get lost, so I borrowed another VHS player and recorded a tape with all of the Ace of Base videos I had by that time on one tape.

I started visiting record stores to get a copy of *The Bridge* album, but I could only find a used copy that I still have. It was phenomenal. I was in love with "My Déjà Vu" and with Jenny's songs, "Ravine" and "Wave Wet Sand." I started wanting to be able to sing their songs properly. I wanted to know the lyrics and what they meant. My older sister (ten years older than me) noticed and she kindly told me she could print the lyrics at her office. She used to work as a reporter at a newspaper and she could print anything she wanted. Ace of Base lyrics were not part of her investigation work, of course, but she managed to make me a book with all of Ace of Base's lyrics. With that book, I started to learn all the songs, but to my surprise there were so many tracks I didn't know… ¿What's "Dr. Sun"? ¿"Captain Nemo"? Is this Ace of Base, or it is a mistake???

I was so curious, but I had little resources to find out. At that time, having the internet at home was expensive and we couldn't afford it. Most people used to go to places called "cyber cafés" to navigate the internet, paying by each hour. I had a computer at home but didn't know how to use it very well, so my younger brother kindly went with me many times to cyber cafés and taught me how to explore the internet where I searched for Ace of Base info every time. I was so surprised to learn that the band released different albums in different territories and even different videos! I remember my brother telling me that I was spending a lot of money on Ace of Base.

Latrer, my brother told me he had heard "Life Is A Flower" on the radio. I called the radio station and requested the song several times. I recorded it on cassette so I could listen to it anytime. The internet was growing fast, but at that time it was so slow, I would have needed hours to save one mp3 file (and I didn't have many downloading skills). I saved my money and paid a friend to burn me a CD with songs he had downloaded with Audio Galaxy or Napster. He had to leave the computer on overnight to save all the songs.

I was so excited to hear the European tracks. Every time I listened to new Ace of Base songs, my love for them grew bigger. I use to post their pictures on my bedroom wall, as desktop wallpapers, in my notebooks, and other places. I put them everywhere! Then I found a cyber café where the internet was a lot faster, and I could finally watch their European videos in RealPlayer... I wanted to have the videos on my computer, so I learned how to save them on diskettes. It wasn't so easy because the files were 5-6MB and diskettes are only 1.4MB. I bought packages of diskettes just so I could save their videos and watch them over and over on my computer at home. With time, I became a lot better at English—and also at computers.

Next Christmas, I asked for the *Flowers* album. It was expensive to buy imported CDs. My parents couldn't believe they would be paying that amount of money "only for a CD" but they knew it meant a lot to me and made an effort so I could have it. I got the UK green version. I played it so much, my brothers ended up hating the band.

In 2000, a difficult part of my life started. I had to go to a new school for the last two years of high school and I found myself in an unfriendly environment. I was starting to feel seriously attracted to other boys, and that is a big problem when you are a teenager who hasn't been educated about it—and you're growing up in a third-world country where discrimination and gay bullying is common. I hid my feelings and acted straight to everyone during my whole adolescence. It felt like being in some kind of jail.

Starting university was also a big struggle. I was happy that I was studying veterinary medicine—my passion, the career that I love—and I concentrated in it. But at the same time, I was sad about myself. Growing up as a gay boy was difficult for me. I wasn't able to tell anyone what I was feeling. I made friends at the university, but I was ashamed and afraid. I also felt guilty and weird about telling them anything personal about me. I even had thoughts of suicide. But I had luck that I was an Acer.

Being an Acer helped me so much at this stage of my life. I used to listen to the band's music when I was feeling sad, and I still do that nowadays. Their music always makes me feel better. But the way they helped me successfully survive that stage goes much deeper than that. Maybe in a way no one can imagine. It was other Acers who helped me. By sharing our love for Ace of Base, I got to know and chat with many people online, not only about Ace of Base, but also about personal struggles that I wasn't able to tell anyone in person.

I was a member of The Hallo Boards, a web forum popular among Acers, and I remember as if it were yesterday. I was reading a post where everyone was sharing their pictures. To my big shock, a male Acer shared a pic of him and his boyfriend hugging each other. I even got scared because I was in a cyber café with people around, so I scrolled fast so no one could see. When I started to read the comments and found replies like, "You look so cute together" and "Congratulations!" I was so surprised that no one was mocking them.

This may be incredible for some people to read, but that moment was the start of my change of views about being gay. It changed the course of my life drastically. It gave me enough courage to chat about what was happening to me with other Acers. Some of them helped me so much to accept myself. Nowadays, I have enough self confidence to be openly gay to everyone and feel proud about it.

I can still remember a *Sounds Nordic* radio interview in 2002 where an Acer asked this question: "A high percentage of your fans are gay. What are your views on homosexuality?" Jenny Berggren answered, "I think that you can have one vision of how it should be until you get to know yourself and other people, and the more you get to know yourself and other people, the more you accept other people and what they think and do. And I think it's very difficult when you don't accept homosexuality, because that is a way of not accepting a way a person is, and I would think that would be a problem." He then asked, "So what do you think of all your gay fans?" And she said, "Well, I love them." Such a great answer for me to hear at that time.

Jenny has always been my favorite member of the band, but after that answer, I loved her even more. I admire her not just because of her beauty or talent but also the down-to-earth way she assumes being a superstar... Songs like "Natural Superstar" and "Beat Of My Heart," which are my personal favorites from her solo album, can clearly illustrate what I'm saying.

Well, from this point, the rest is history. I finished university, got a degree as a veterinarian, found a partner, and opened up to my parents, family, and friends. And, as soon as I started working and earning my own money, I became an Ace of Base collector. My goal was to get at least one version of every commercial single and every album—and I did!

At first, it was easier to collect Ace of Base stuff, but as my country's economy started to fall down and many government restrictions appeared, it was difficult to keep collecting. I couldn't buy any more items from online shops or from other countries (even having enough money) because of legal restrictions. But that didn't stop me. I started trading stuff by mail and I even got Jenny's solo album through one of my clients at the veterinary clinic. My client mentioned that a relative would travel to Sweden. Who would have thought I would have someone in my consult with a relative that would travel to Sweden? I was so lucky! I asked them to help me get the *My Story* album—and they did! Her relative kindly took the time to search for it in Sweden. Such a nice person. She mentioned it wasn't easy to find. At the store, they were so surprised to hear that the CD was for someone in Venezuela.

Nowadays, I can bet I have the biggest collection in Venezuela. It is not as big as other collections around the world, but I'm extremely proud of it because I got it with my biggest effort and, of course, with the kind help of many Acers all over the world. I keep my collection as a treasure that represents a life that would have been so different if this music didn't exist. Also, many items are like a token of friendship with many Acers.

I feel blessed to say I have met a lot of good people and great friends through Ace of Base. I know there are many great artists in the world, but no other could have had a bigger influence in my life. Somehow, I feel that everything that has happened would never have been the same if it wasn't for this band I love.

Right now, at the moment I'm writing this, I'm planning to make a big change in my life that may not have been possible without the help of the incredibly generous and great people I have met in Jenny's and Ace of Base's fandom.

I have many dreams and personal goals to reach at this point of my life, and one of the things I wish the most is to see Jenny in concert and meet her in person just to say thank you. And to let her know how positive her existence has been in my life.

I would also like to meet face to face with as many of the online Acer friends as I can. Thanks to many of them, I still have faith that humanity can triumph in this crazy world, and I feel I have become a better person.

Another one of my goals is to be able to help others as they have helped me. And that's one of the reasons I wanted to be a part of this project. I hope it gets to help many people.

And Jenny, if you're reading this: I wish you the most happy life someone could ever have. Thanks for making mine a lot happier!

Elio posing with one of the many exotic creatures he meets at work

ABOUT THE AUTHOR: Elio lives in Maracaibo, Venezuela and works at Zulia State University as a veterinary surgery professor. He is passionate about exotic animal medicine and entomology. His favorite Jenny Berggren songs are "He Decides," "Wave Wet Sand," "Beat Of My Heart," and "Give Me The Faith." He also loves Jenny's version of Lisa Nilsson's "Varje Gång Jag Ser Dig." His favorite Ace of Base songs include "Change With The Light" and "The Sign." He won a signed test-pressing of the *Hidden Gems* LP in 2015, the same day his mom was scheduled to undergo major surgery. Receiving such happy news during a stressful situation made him feel that nothing could go wrong that day. You can contact Elio at elio_carrillo@hotmail.com.

236

Never Lose Hope

by Carlos Santiago

Ace of Base came into my life at a precise moment—when I was in middle school and nothing was easy. I might say that it was the hardest time at school. I remember back in those days, and specially the day when everything started…

In middle school, it is common to have festivals, and each grade is required to create a performance to show their parents. Our grade chose to perform a rhythmic dance, but we didn't have a song, so a group of girls were given the job of choosing one. They brought three tapes to class. They played each song and we had to pick one as a group. I cannot even recall which songs they were, but one caught my attention. I was not used to listening to music in English, but my interest in music in English began that day. Rehearsals started, and the more I listened to that song, the more I got myself hooked.

Due to the lack of internet during those years, it was difficult to know about that new band, where they came from, and who they were, but did that really matter? I guess not because that song was stuck in my head. Finally, I knew what the song was called: "The Sign." I wanted so badly to know a little more about that album, so one day during rehearsals, the cassette sat beside the tape recorder. I grabbed it for just a second to know the band's name. There it was: Ace of Base.

One day, I was walking in a market when suddenly, I heard "The Sign." I tried to locate where the music was coming from and ran to the CD stand. I knew it was time to buy the CD. But since I had been grounded for bad grades that month, all my money had been taken away. So I ran to my house and begged my mom for my money back. I guess I was thinking it was the last album and soon the stand would run out of CDs. My mom accepted under the condition I get better grades (and if I didn't, something worse would happen). So, I ran back to the stand and bought the album. I didn't know how to play it because it was my first CD. I had the idea that I had to flip it back as a vinyl. I was the happiest person in the entire world.

As time passed, I gathered more information. Not so much, but enough. I even thought they were Americans! The Berggren siblings and their lifelong friend made my life easier with their music. When everything was wrong at school, and I had to cope with those abusive boys, I just thought of a beautiful melody and let the things go away. I knew it wouldn't be forever.

In a little time, all the bands and the music I listened to were replaced by Ace of Base. It is true that we were delighted with that blonde girl called Linn in the beginning, but there was another member on vocals: her sister Jenny, and why didn't she deserve some credit too?

One day, I was listening to the radio in the morning and I heard something important. The DJ was talking about the new Ace of Base album, so I asked for the CD as a birthday present. *The Bridge* album is something magnificent and awesome with grand quality. With the second album, I started focusing on Jenny and understood the word magic. If I can choose a word to express everything they have done, that word has to be *magic*. Both made magic. There is no other explanation of what they did together.

The band came to Mexico, my country, for their first and only time. That was awesome! I could see them on TV. As a teenager, I never thought of going to the airport or things like that. (How foolish can someone be when young?)

I was in high school on my first day when I heard their new single "Cruel Summer." So immediately, I went to search for the new album. I had grown up by then and could travel alone on the streets. When I saw the *Cruel Summer* album, I jumped up out of happiness. I realized with their third album that Jenny had grown as a singer. She overcame that horrible experience with that crazy fan. She took responsibility in leading the band. With this new step, I loved Jenny's work even more and she immediately began to be my favorite Ace.

Unfortunately, their music started to be played less frequently on the American continent. I knew that there was new music in Europe. I tried to get those new singles with no luck—until one morning. Back then, I started classes at 9:00 a.m. I was sleeping that morning when my sister came running into my room screaming, "C'est la vie!" "C'est la vie!" "C'est la vie!" I knew perfectly what that meant. I jumped down from the bed and ran quickly to the stereo, took a tape, and began recording.

The recording was incomplete, but I listened and listened to it over and over. I couldn't listen any more times because I had classes, and then I had to go to work. Damn, how could that be possible on my first day of work? I wanted to return home and have more listens.

No words can explain what I experienced that day. It is unspeakable. That day, November 11th is one of the most representative memories in my life, so I decided to get a tattoo: 11:11 It represents that month and day, and each "number one" (or bar) represents a band member.

The *Da Capo* era was so minimal. There was no promotion or singles on the radio. I thought it was the end. Unfortunately, bad choices were made in the band. In 2010, I had the opportunity to meet Jonas and Ulf. I was disappointed because there would be only two members on this most expected day when my dream was to meet all of them.

Something new came, and having the *My Story* album was the best reward to heal all the wounds. Jenny was active again as a solo singer and she showed us that the fans would never be alone. The *My Story* album is definitely Jenny's work—each song has something special and a deep meaning. All the effort she put in is clearly noticeable.

Jenny started doing concerts in many parts of the world, so I thought my moment to attend must be coming soon. One day, it was announced that she would perform in Minneapolis, Minnesota, USA. It was the opportunity I had been waiting for after more than twenty years. Unfortunately, it was never confirmed.

But everything changed a month later when Jenny announced a concert in Lima, Peru. It was the new opportunity I had been waiting for again. I cannot explain all the feelings I had. Many Acers and I were a little skeptical about this concert. Still, I thought, "Let's do it and reach for this goal." I took a risk and booked flight tickets and a hotel for just a weekend in Lima, Peru.

The day came and I arrived early at the airport. I waited for another Acer friend. We flew more than five hours to Lima and got in touch with more Acers that had arrived for the same reason. It was a wonderful moment to see in front of me such well-known faces, and some new ones too. Acers from Peru, Chile, Argentina, Colombia, Brazil, Ecuador, and Mexico would attend her concert. We were there for the same purpose: to finally make our dream come true.

At 2:00 a.m., we arrived at the hotel (fortunately, it was easy to find all the right places with the help of the Peruvian Acers). Minutes turned to hours. We were nervous, tired. My hair was a mess because of the humidity, but what did it matter? After a long wait, finally two SUVs appeared, and yes! There she was! I will never forget how she came to see us and how kind she was. She gave us time to have stuff signed, take pictures, and share some words. She is an amazing person! I expected just a little and she gave a lot.

We returned back to our hotels, and the following morning, we went to take a tour of downtown. We were buying some sodas because of the hot weather when suddenly, Jenny appeared walking in front of us. That was a miracle that we had found her again a few hours later. She took just a picture with all of us because she was on her way to give an interview at a radio station.

At night, we were ready to enjoy our first concert. Again, the wait was so long, and when I saw her on stage singing for us, it was totally incredible. The only thing that was important to me was the concert.

I don't know if it was coincidence or what happened to me, but during "The Sign" I couldn't hold back my tears. Maybe because "The Sign" was the first song I ever listened to. I was so excited, and that was my moment. The concert continued with great acceptance, and in the end, she held a meet & greet. What an amazing experience!

Jenny continued with concerts. Next stop: Houston, Texas, USA. I was ready for it. Unfortunately, things didn't work, but having met such wonderful people again and attending an Acer Meeting there was so great.

Then another concert: Mexico City, my city. I needed to attend that concert. Having Jenny singing in my country would be priceless.

We had a really nice meet & greet before the concert where she told us about her experience in Teotihuacán, a famous archaeological zone in Mexico.

Again, Jenny was so humble and nice and gave each of us a gift of a signed picture. All fans behaved properly with her, and I guess she felt very comfortable with us. During the concert, she was very well-accepted by the crowd. People were singing, jumping, and clapping hands. And she performed "Natural Superstar."

The last concert I could attend was in Chicago, Illinois, USA. Again, a tired weekend but to meet new Acers again and have a good time with the others I met in Houston was excellent. I enjoyed every single song Jenny performed. I only regret the little time I spent in Chicago.

There are no borders in music. With the music, we are a big family. No matter where you are from and no matter what language you speak, music keeps us united.

All these experiences have taught me how to become a better person in life. They taught me to be humble and to reach goals. There is no bigger block than the ones you build in your head. Jenny Berggren also helped me to be persistent. Never leave what you love. Never lose faith. This is my story.

Carlos and Jenny at the meet & greet in Lima, Peru (2017)

ABOUT THE AUTHOR: Carlos lives in Tlalnepantla, State of Mexico, Mexico. He loves to enjoy a tasty meal and, of course, the pleasure of listening to good music. His biggest passion is to travel anywhere to experience new places, cultures, and food. There is no reason for Carlos to sit and rest inside all day. He ventures out instead. His favourite solo songs from Jenny are "Beat Of My Heart" and "Numb."

Do You Know This Feeling?

by Masha Kalodka

Do you know this feeling, when you get goosebumps and it's cold, and at the same time, it seems as if you are thrown into a heat? When the goosebumps are so strong and so big that it seems they will continue on forever, and they completely control your body. Squeeze, enthrall, hit the heart, cause delight and tears, and they run, run huge jolts all over your body… Do you know?

This was my feeling on the 2 of June 2018 at Jenny's concert in Minsk when I heard a story about her father, about two coins, bread, and a flower. A story about Love and the song "Don't Turn Around." I cried, although I usually don't cry when I'm with people—and even less so from songs. But I could not restrain myself. Only a very talented and sincere person is able to give such feelings and tears and such emotions. It was touching, and I think it was an exchange of warmth, of hearts.

Only a singer who knows what she is singing about—and only a person who has experienced pain can do that. It seems to me that she has seen pain, and I heard it in her voice sometimes. It's not just lyrics. It's all from the bottom of the heart, from inside. It's a part of the soul.

244

Emotions were strong that day, and I don't really remember the next few songs. I only remember her eyes. They were sometimes sad, sometimes laughing, and also happy. There were lights in them. They are alive.

I was not a fan and I went to a concert. Just a concert of a famous band. BUT! I was fond of her music and soul during the concert. I fell in love with her voice, her eyes, with her real and sincere emotions that night. I fell in love not with a singer, but with a person who sings beautifully.

Later, after the concert, I looked through a large number of interviews I could find in English or with a translation. At the concert, I did not know that she had such a beautiful soul. I only felt it intuitively. And after watching interviews at home, I realized that my intuition was right. She has a rich soul. And I became more and more interested in discovering Jenny's world.

I also listened to all the songs I could find. Some of my favourites are "Give Me The Faith," "The Sky Proclaims Your Glory," "Numb," and "Dying To Stay Alive." These songs give me strength and peace, tranquility and confidence. They are my support. And with "Dying To Stay Alive," I start my mornings with it. I dance along to it at the start of each new day.

For me, Jenny has become a teacher in many ways. Yes, she might not know it, but her dream of becoming a teacher came true in this way. In many of her answers to the questions, she teaches us to treat life correctly. Jenny talks about herself, she works hard improving herself. And this is a huge motivation for us, for the audience, just to work on ourselves. This subject is much more complicated and interesting than any school subject. Be yourself, be able to take what happens and move in the right direction.

In an interview in Israel, she said: "I enjoy being me… Hope you enjoy being you." I am trying, trying to do it. And Jenny helps me. Even at a distance and without knowing her, it is possible. Jenny has become a source of inspiration and happiness. I am comfortable in her world.

Thank you, Jenny!

I hope one day I will be able to meet her eyes face to face and be able to say thank you in person.

Masha is fond of music and theater, which are important parts of her life

ABOUT THE AUTHOR: Masha is a native of Minsk, Belarus and a lawyer in business law. She is twenty seven, but always twenty one. She likes to discover new things, meet people, travel, and learn about the world. She dreams of going on a round-the-world trip someday. She is an optimist and believes that, as Jenny says, life is worth living. Some of her other favourite songs from Jenny are, "Beautiful Morning," "All Hope," "Free Me," and, of course, "Don't Turn Around." Her Instagram is @marusia_vla

Eight Years to the Sounds of My Story

by Julia Kozina

November 2010

After Jenny's album release, I quit my job. To be more exact, it happened thanks to her song "Gotta Go." I know this song has its meaning, but its lyrics influenced me in their own way. I think everyone understands every song differently, and it often makes us change something, gives us a call to action.

I hated my job. I also hated Mondays. The beginning of the week meant I had to get up and go to hell. Yes, that's how I entered the office every morning. I entered hell at 9:00 a.m. I had the possibility to escape for lunch between 1:00-2:00 p.m. And at 6:00 p.m., I broke free. I particularly looked forward to 6:00 p.m. at the end of the week because Friday meant freedom. It sounds unhealthy and harsh, but that's how every day of my life was then. The office, from co-founders to low-level positions, was as dumb as possible. However, our design and advertising department was quite normal. There were some creative and ambitious people there, which led to staff turnover. But the manager of our department still remains an example for me—an example of an unprofessional petty tyrant. I managed to work in this loony bin for two and a half years!

Yes, I know it's not the most horrible thing that can happen in life, and maybe I shouldn't overdramatize it. But when your mental state is close to clinical depression, maybe you should start raising the alarm in time? The worst thing I felt during that time was insecurity, an awful feeling. It kills everything. So I went to a psychologist for the first time. It helped.

Run away, run away means nothing
When you've lost your goal
Gotta push it another level,
Retain control
Don't waste your time

I shouldn't have wasted my time. We often waste our time trying to please others, and when we do, we lose ourselves. And at the end of our lives, we realize we haven't lived at all—and the worst thing is maybe we don't get one more chance. So sad. That's why when life gives you the signs, you should pay attention to them so you don't feel sad later. That's why this song, and the release of my favourite singer's album, made me start a new life.

Six months earlier, I thought about my dismissal on that warm evening in Stockholm when I was alone. Half a year had passed, but I still remember this magic evening as if it was happening to me now: In the evening, I'm sitting at the sea promenade not far from city hall. The sun's warm, the heat's away. Soft shadows are covering the streets. The city's slowly sinking into the twilight. The summer's been hot, probably in all of Europe. There was a hell of smog and a smell of burning in Moscow for several weeks. It's more than 25°C here. That's rare for Stockholm. I feel so free and happy.

A few days later, after Jenny's concert in Kristianopel, I thought about my dismissal again. Of course, I didn't tell her anything about my situation. I would never do that. We talked about other things. She just has a special energy, very positive. You look at such people

249

and catch their wave. But to stay on this wave, you need to change something about yourself. I needed to stop fearing.

I had been afraid of something since childhood. Many of these fears were taught by my parents, of course in good faith. When you have a late and long-awaited child, you'll always be protecting her. At that time, I was afraid of quitting "to nowhere." Of becoming destitute, of being labeled as jobless, of ruining my CV, of not building a career. As I'm writing it, I realize how stupid it was, but everything seemed serious to me then. Money makes us the prisoners of circumstance; we get used to it, it becomes our drug. Of course, one needs to work and earn money, but your job must bring you pleasure, develop you. If it doesn't, don't waste your time ("Gotta Go").

After my dismissal, I had free time. And for the last six months, I managed to save enough money to exist after my dismissal. I received an invitation to a new job, but my start was scheduled for January 2011, so I decided to go to Sweden to attend one of Jenny's concerts in Alingsås.

December 2010. Sweden. Alingsås.

Alingsås is a small, cosy town close to Gothenburg. The whole town is decorated for Christmas. It's -3°C and snowing. It's so calm and cosy.

Jenny's church concert has just finished. I sit drinking coffee, and I talk to Jenny and Jakob until the lights turn out. Then I understand—it's time to go. We say goodbye by the car. They travel to Gothenburg. I return to the hotel and sit in my room drinking tea.

I have to get up early the next day, but I don't want to sleep. Snowflakes are falling outside the window. I hear the sound of Christmas songs (probably from the neighboring room). It's so calm around and I understand that everything is the way it should be. That this is true happiness. Happiness is in the little things: There's a perfect winter outside, I've got fresh bed linen, and my favourite singer released a new album two months ago that gave me strength to break out of the deadlock.

In January 2011, I start my new job at a small advertising agency.

January 2013. Moscow.
Unfortunately, our small advertising agency failed. I worked there for two years until it closed. We had a great team, and the fact we don't work together anymore doesn't prevent us from getting together every month. We jokingly call it a meeting of the "Fired Club."

I've been looking for a job for half a year. I've started working in three places. I haven't stayed anywhere for a long time because back in 2010, I had promised myself I would never ever work anywhere I felt uncomfortable again.

In the summer of 2013, I started studying studio photography and Adobe Lightroom. I almost decided to make photography my business, but I didn't and that's good. There were fewer orders at that time. My courses were in the evening, so I started painting in my free time. I don't remember how it happened the first time, but I just decided to paint something.

There's a great classic education in Russia in the field of drawing, painting, composition, color theory, plastic anatomy, etc. but it completely ruins your fantasy. Sometimes I wanted to draw something, but my heart skipped a bit in front of an empty sheet, in fear of getting it dirty. Many artists have a fear of the white paper.

I remember opening my sketchbook for the first time and turning on "Free Me" to escape the fear of the white paper. I just started drawing a line. Since then, I've been painting. Sometimes I take a break. Sometimes I paint for days without distracting myself from the canvas, but the fact is—I paint! I make all my fantasies come true; I depict them on the canvas. My art is my diary, my desires, my dreams.

Now I prefer good A4 watercolour paper and pencils. I draw or paint when I want to. I don't force myself. I paint to get it on fabric. Who knows? Maybe someday I'll risk starting my own accessory line. I'd like to say that *My Story* has inspired me to start painting again.

24 November 2015.
My dad passed away. He started feeling ill at night and was taken to the hospital.

It was a heart attack.

I still remember his look. He was winking at me and he tried to smile, but it was a sad smile. He smiled goodbye. In the morning, Mom called and told me he's gone.

I couldn't cry. It was all a blur. Then there was the funeral—and a year that was quite tough. Now I understand when they say one needs a year to accept the death of someone close to you.

Day by day, you live through all the four seasons: every month, every week, every day, every hour, every minute, every second, every moment without this person. It can be quite hard, but it's necessary for accepting the fact itself.

Throughout the year, there were a lot of moments of desperation, tears, apathy. But the closer to the anniversary, the easier it was. During the hard times, these helped me most of all: deadlines at work, I adopted a cat (I don't understand how I could live without it before), and Jenny's songs that I heard for the first time.

On the day my father died, Jenny released a song in Swedish: "Så Skimrande Var Aldrig Havet" (for the Swedish TV show *Så Mycket Bättre*). As I understand, Jenny dedicated this song to her father who also died. It happened that I first heard this song on the day of my father's death.

I could not listen to this song for a long time. It was hard. But somewhere in those eight months, I listened to it by accident. The song was in my playlist. Before, I ignored it and switched to the next song. The song caused me tears and memories. But that day, I decided to listen to it. Tears no longer existed. Time heals wounds. Now when I hear this song, it makes me smile sadly.

The song that helped me a lot was "Dying to Stay Alive":

You know, I'm dying to stay alive
When everything is breaking down
You've got a choice to make it new

It can have another meaning, but then I've been rediscovering it as if it was sung to me. I've been listening to Jenny's other songs too, but this one most often. It's really becoming easier. From this song, it was easier. It's a dance song, but the words can be heard in different ways. I was in a situation of total despair. But listening to this song, I realized that life goes on. I realized that it was hurting now, but I understood that I must continue to live.

One month after my father's death, I decided to visit Jenny's concert because I'd already bought the tickets and my friend was waiting for me (even though she understood what could make me stay home). But I decided to go because life goes on. And we are the continuation of our parents. When they leave, a part of them keeps staying alive inside of us—"Dying to Stay Alive."

Now I take his death easier; I've accepted it as something inevitable. We have so much to lose ahead. And someday, our day will come, the day when we leave this world. Until this day, we have time—time for our lives. It's up to us to decide how we spend it, our life.

2017-2018

I visited Jenny's concert in Tula (Russia) with my friends in August 2017. After the concert, we had a short meeting with Jenny and I asked her a question about her church concerts in Sweden. I asked my question in English. She replied that she had no church concerts planned at the moment. And she said with a smile, "Wow! Julia, do you speak English?!" I answered: "Yes, sometimes." She said: "Your English is good!"

I was pleased, but I know that my English is not very good. But after her words, I decided to learn English again. This is my fourth attempt. I started to learn the language three times before. First it was interesting, but then it became boring. I started to study on my own. I listened to podcasts in English and spent a lot of time reading in English. It gave a little result. I started to talk in English.

January 13, 2018, I was at Jenny's concert in Kazan (Tatarstan, a subject of the Russian Federation). After the concert, I had a meeting with Jenny about half an hour long. I could talk to her in English. It was my little victory. Before, I used to need friends' help in translation. Now I continue to learn English and I really like this language!

I want to start learning Swedish in parallel. I've been to Sweden many times. I really love this country, its culture, and its people. Sweden taught me how to love nature. I'll never get bored with going there.

During these eight years, there have been many events in my life—sad and merry. Jenny's songs have been with me these eight years and they stay with me. The *My Story* album, these are the best songs for me.

Over the years, I have changed myself. I became more cynical, closed, selfish, but more tolerant, calm, and self-confident. I began to feel calm about my appearance. I realized that I can't be good for everyone, and I don't want to be. You need to appreciate those people who appreciate you. And I do not plan for the future. I realized one important truth: it is necessary to live in the moment.

Everyone has come to this world with some purpose. Someone is going to become very famous, someone is going to be a really good parent, some can sing, some can paint, some are going to travel all over the world, some are going to write books, etc. And that's great! But no one knows how long we are going to stay in this world. Everyone has their time. When life gives you the chance, take it. Live in the moment because tomorrow might never come.

Julia chatting with Jenny after a church performance

ABOUT THE AUTHOR: Julia is a graphic designer from Moscow, Russia. She adores travel, sunrises and sunsets, nature, photography, painting, movies, music, Sweden (and all things Swedish), AOB, and Jenny Berggren. And her own creations, which provide inspiration too.

Full Circle

by Trace Adam

When I was a high school student in the late 2000s, I was definitely the only Ace of Base fan in my school. It's not surprising. None of the others grew up with Ace of Base's music like I did. *The Sign* is the first album I ever owned. I listened to both that album and *The Bridge* throughout my childhood. My mom still often recalls me singing "The Sign" as a toddler with a portable karaoke machine cassette player I had in the living room.

I now remix and produce music on a professional level. And the first songs I ever tried to remix were Ace of Base songs using rudimentary software before I even entered my teens. The music I was making at that time was quite basic, but it was the beginning of my biggest passion.

A few years later, in my early teens, I turned to the internet for a way to connect and talk about Ace of Base's music with others. I felt a bit out of place, as it seemed like all the other fans online were at much different stages in their lives. Still, in what would last for years, I began to use The AceBoards forum to talk about news, the possibilities of new music, and the tour.

I shared some of my early remixes, which were slowly getting better the more I learned. I began to delve deeper into their discography and fell in love with the *Cruel Summer* album. Learning about Linn's disappearance and the way it was handled got me even more intrigued. Soon, however, I quickly realized that part of being an Ace of Base fan is learning how to withstand a lot of waiting (for magic). Even so, there were plenty of demos, b-sides, and other tracks that seemed "new" to me to keep me occupied along the way.

Then, in early 2010, a new song finally appeared—a Jenny song. "Free Me" was the first new studio recording that we had with Jenny's vocals in years (not counting the remakes). And to me, it felt like having a new Ace of Base song. It was like getting a late Christmas present, and I was ecstatic. The video was cool, dark, and exciting (I'm still hoping we'll get the full version someday). The album was at last released in late 2010, close to the release of *The Golden Ratio*.

It was a trying time to be a fan. On one hand, we got two fantastic but vastly different albums. But on the other hand, we had two different parties of our favorite band clearly disagreeing, to put it lightly. I followed the situation closely and it was a bittersweet circumstance.

My Story has become one of my all-time favorite albums. It has some of the best written pop music I've ever listened to, and Jenny's vocals sound like they've been used to her best ability. It's dark sounding at times, but it's also very smart and concise. Jenny showcases strong, inspired vocals that are the best she's ever sounded. It's easy to tell that the album was a true labor of love for her.

My Story is incredibly well thought out, polished, and still sounds modern even now, years after its release. The album has been a huge influence in some of my most recent remix productions.

My Story was released at a time when I was just entering adulthood. Everything came full circle. Ace of Base's music, and by extension Jenny, has guided me literally throughout my entire life. The production work on both Jenny's and Ace of Base's material has shaped how I want my music to sound. Their cheerful, upbeat lyricism has allowed me to forget about difficult times, think positively, and follow my dreams—and I owe them a debt of gratitude for that.

Trace created the edit for the "Would You Believe" music video (2015)

ABOUT THE AUTHOR: Trace Adam lives in New York, USA. He can typically be found spending hours producing remixes of Britney Spears songs, among other artists. His favorite song from Jenny is "Spend This Night" and one of his biggest aspirations is to produce an official Jenny remix someday. You can find him on Facebook: traceadam, Instagram: @traceadam, and YouTube: traceadamremixes.

Be Someone

by Sara West

"Be a Jenny!" Lindsay yelled across the ice. "Huh? WHAT?" I yelled back. "You can do it! Be a Jenny!" she repeated.

Lindsay and I had become fast friends during our study year abroad in Sweden. We both had the same taste in music. And we both loved adventure and trying new experiences. She lived near a town called Mora and I ended up in Gothenburg.

On this December day, I was hoping for a new adventure while visiting her in Mora. I mentioned ice skating, so we decided to locate a suitable surface in the woods near her host family's home. "I don't have skates," I said as Lindsay half-smirked. "You can borrow some from my host brother. You said you wanted to try it, right?" She was right. I wanted to give it a go and she was offering, so we ventured into the subarctic chill.

I laced up a pair of ill-fitting hockey skates and wobbled over to the edge of the pond. I planted my feet, stood upright, and duck walked my way forward before falling into a snowbank near the edge of the ice. Lindsay skated up beside me and snickered. I pushed myself back up and step-skated across the center once again.

Ice skating looked so charming and cozy on TV. Reality turned out to be less than comfortable. Five minutes later, the chill had numbed my face, my feet, and my resolve. No more for me. I was done!

As I tapped my way back to the edge, Lindsay yelled something in my direction, but the distance made it impossible to hear. So she repeated the phrase with the big impact: "Be a Jenny!"

Lindsay—and all my other friends—used the phrase to great effect. Hearing them say it helped me do things I didn't think I could do. It helped keep me going when things became too much to handle.

When I heard her yell it across the pond that day, I laughed and echoed back, "Be a Jenny!" Her encouragement renewed my determination and we ice skated for thirty more minutes before returning to the warm glow of the fireplace at her host family's home.

That phrase held promise and unlimited potential in my mind. I could do anything. I could be anything. I didn't have to be quiet or shy or anxious. I could escape everything I disliked about myself. All I needed to do was be a Jenny—the singing sensation Jenny. The Jenny who was outgoing, smart, funny, fearless, charismatic, engaging, and talented.

I could be a perfect, sociable, extroverted person like her if I tried. So I worked hard every day to be outgoing, talkative, and well-spoken.

Before long, that phrase of encouragement from friends morphed into a personal burden of my own making. An imperative followed by an insult I often mumbled to myself: "Be a Jenny! You stupid, foolish girl!" Despite all my effort, I could never get things right and was always saying things wrong.

One day, I needed to make a short phone call, so I picked up the receiver and began dialing: seven, one, three... I hung up in the middle of the process. Hesitating, I dialed again: seven, one, three, three... Click. Studying the numbers, I willed myself to dial a third time. "I can do this. I can do this." This third attempt also ended in failure.

And so it went. Dialing the same number and hanging up. Click. Click. Click. Click. Every new attempt a self-sabotage. Every new attempt ending in a sickly combination of nausea, tears, and sweat. On the cusp my nineteenth birthday, I spent two hours in this spiral. It took everything I had to dial and stay on the line for a two-minute call. It was here—at this exact moment—that I knew my life had gone off the rails.

Somehow and somewhere, my shyness and anxiety, which had been a nuisance in years past, had grown into a swirling malicious source of constant dread. Interacting with other people meant never-ending waves of warm, intense fear that ruled my life.

And here was the real proof I could never be a Jenny. I could never be what I saw in her. I could only be what I had within me. And what did I have? Nothing. An echoing, cavernous space full of nothing gnawing away at my being.

I have nothing here within me.

I hated that line. Hearing Jenny sing it in "Give Me The Faith" felt dumb and untrue. *She has nothing within her?? What does she mean?! She has everything I want!* I thought in protest.

A nagging internal whisper remained, "What if it's true? What if there is nothing there within her?" It would mean Jenny was not who I thought she was. It would mean she wasn't a hero. Worse, it would mean she was flawed and incomplete. I couldn't accept that. Understand it? I could do that. I could understand her humanity in my mind. It doesn't mean I accepted it, "If my hero is flawed, what hope do I have?" my reasoning went.

No, but in you is everything.

I hated that line too. How I hated that line! It was a baseball bat to the face because it represented yet another thing Jenny had that I didn't—God himself. In an interview in 1998, she told a story about staying in a Montreal hotel room. The story went something like this: She was lonely, so she asked God to show up, and he did. It seemed like such a simple thing. You have a problem, you ask for the solution, and God is there to help. How convenient and, frankly, unfair.

"Why does she get that and I don't? That's not fair! I want that too!" I thought. When I realized I *could* get that too, I violently pulled away. Excuses rushed through my mind: "I have no idea who God is. My anxiety is too much. I'm not ready. I can't trust him. I just can't."

The biggest hinder was my fear—a fear that those lyrics might be true. What if the song *is right?* What if everything *is* in him? Agreeing to such a statement has deep, life-changing repercussions.

I cautiously approached this triune God, running away when he felt too close. Still curious, I would tiptoe up, sneak a glimpse, and steal away. Some days, I would want to be near but was too stubborn, or too weak, to make an effort. That's when songs from Jenny and Jakob helped create an opening—a pinpoint of light in the dark. Their songs pushed through my defenses and built a bridge over my confusion. Songs like "Tvivel," "Att Vara Rädd," "All Hope," "Look at the Cross," and "Herrens Sanning" opened up new perspectives and new paths to a Father, Son, and Holy Spirit I barely knew.

BE SOMEONE

I ignored, forgot, remembered, and returned to God with fearful, rotating consistency for nearly five years. Finally, one night I ran so close, I saw the everything—my eyes wide to the awe. That's when I knew "Give Me The Faith" and all the other songs were true. After that, my empty desire to be a perfect pop star dissipated. It turns out filling a deep void is possible when you have access to everything. I became more confident, more laid-back, and less anxious. I could make a phone call without issue and interact without dread.

Jenny turned from hero to role model in my mind: an intelligent, creative, faithful person full of integrity and joy. "I could still learn a thing or two from someone like that," I thought as I ordered a copy of her autobiography *Vinna Hela Världen* in 2009.

Its pages revealed the inside story behind the voice on the albums, the face on the screen. An all-access pass into the winding, blinding corridors of fame: a whirlwind tour of one person's journey through a life lived in unusual circumstances. Fans were excited about it, and rightly so. Critics in Sweden wrote positive reviews, which was nearly a miracle all its own. Anything connected to Ace of Base was usually dragged through the dirt by reviewers. Not this time. It received strong support across the board. Her book left many readers with a feeling of peace and contentment after finishing the final page. I finished it and felt like shit.

Page after page and chapter after chapter, I compared. The role model and me. The woman of faith and me. I was small again—seventeen-year-old "Be a Jenny" small.

This woman of great faith traipsed through the pages, breezed through the hard parts. She made it look easy. Her trust in God felt outsized.

I was exasperated. "How does she *do that?*" I wondered. "I could never hope to be half that." She always ran toward God while I was stuck with a prodigal habit of running the other direction. Old insecurities, newly packaged: I wasn't good enough. I could never measure up. I was quite simply useless.

"Here I Am," the first radio single from *My Story*, appeared shortly after the book. The song title echoed a phrase used by several people in the Bible when God called on them to give of themselves. "That's the difference between us," I thought, "She says *'Here I Am!'* while I say, *'Me?! No Thanks'.*"

Later that year, Anja and Jessi, two good friends and co-creators of The Jenny Source, ventured to Sweden to gather media content during the release of *My Story*. They kindly invited me to tag along, so I packed a bag and joined their adventure.

The adventure brought us to cities big and small where we watched Jenny captivate audiences with her voice and story. It saw us traveling by taxi through Stockholm where our favorite singer spontaneously burst into song from the front passenger seat. It's where we watched journalist after journalist interview her about her music. It's where she split one sandwich four ways to share it with us. And where she gave each of us a personal copy of her first solo album.

Our adventure continued the next day. Jenny was scheduled to take part in Förkväll, a live TV show, and we were invited. The three of us arrived at the TV studio (or what we thought was the right studio) when a receptionist broke the news, "Jenny and her musicians left about thirty minutes ago," she said and continued, "the Förkväll studio is in central Stockholm. You'll need to go back the way you came." We rushed back to the car and returned to the traffic jam we had just left.

The sun dipped below the horizon outside the correct building as an intern greeted us on the first floor, "Welcome! We're still filming. Let's take the elevator up to the studio."

At the end of the studio hallway, someone sat alone on a low seat looking small and nervous: face tense, anxiety evident, one hand squeezing the other in an act of self-soothing. My eyes silently asked a question and my head tilted in tandem. A dozen thoughts spilled in every direction. I recognized her and I didn't. I caught one anonymous glance before Jenny looked up. Her face transformed into a warm smile when she saw the three of us.

At 6:10 p.m., Jenny was live-on-air with the nation's eyes upon her. As Sweden watched, Jessi and Anja took photos while I roamed the backstage area. As I took in the sensory experience of touring a TV studio for the first time, I took in the mental experience of recognizing myself in Jenny for the first time. She had been small and anxious. Turned inward toward herself. For a second, I saw it: for a second, she had been like me.

In my head, I knew she had experienced nervousness before. It's not a new phenomenon for anyone. If you're alive, you've been nervous. Even so, seeing her like that created a type of emotional discord within me. To know is one thing; to see another.

This marked the beginning of a third view: the real one. Jenny as a person. Someone like me. Someone like you. Someone who is doing the best they can with what they have. Who is happy and sad and anxious in different measure. Who gets bruised, hurt, broken, torn along the path of living. Who wants to do good but doesn't always hit the mark. Someone who loves, who loses, who forgives, who is forgiven. Someone who experiences both joy and pain, sometimes at the same time.

Once the show wrapped, we dipped back into the lobby and found a comfortable set of chairs on the second floor to talk *My Story*. A full day had passed since Jenny gifted us copies and she wanted to know what we thought. She sat on the edge of the chair, placing her hands on her knees, elbows out and leaning forward. "So, what do you think?" she asked. Her eyes childlike, curious. She craved connection. The opportunity for someone to hear and acknowledge her. "How human," I thought, "how completely human."

When I complimented her on "Going Home," her face brightened and she sat up straighter. At one point I said, "'Beat Of My Heart' doesn't click with me." A tinge of disappointment flashed across her face as she realized the track didn't connect with this particular listener. During our chat, she explained the creative process behind the album, her voice rising with excitement as she spoke. She cared what people thought, and it showed.

Our Sweden-wide adventures ebbed to a close later that week. I stuffed my belongings, souvenirs, and a new view into my suitcase in preparation for my return home. Once back, I listened to the album more deeply. I learned that *My Story* pulses with solemn, honest, driven, and gritty tracks. It's a piece of art strewn with hurt and heartache, embroidered with streaming bursts of joy and light along the edges. It includes tension and trial mixed with hope and healing—a relatable, honest telling of a person's life.

The songs didn't feel anything like the paragraphs in *Vinna Hela Världen*. The woman in those pages breezed through the book with ease. The woman singing these songs wasn't breezing through anything. No, it was more like stumbling forward instead. It confused me since the album was said to be a compliment to the book. The comparison just didn't make sense, so I went back to those pages. What had I missed? The whole point, it turns out.

For the first time, I read the book as intended. Not the imagined book about the hero or the role model. The real book about the real person living a real life. The same person I encountered before the live TV broadcast. This time, all her brokenness was apparent and easy to spot. The mess, the misgivings, the mistakes were there written from cover to cover. It turns out the book and album follow the same complementary pattern: a person living, loving, trying, hoping, hurting, healing, growing, and being.

I re-read the chapter about her time in Montreal when she asked God for help. The simple story of a small problem solved was not so simple in reality. Reading back over the chapter was a suffocatingly real experience: a woman mentally running back and forth ignoring the things that would help her. Trying everything under her own power to fix herself. Trying to sit still. Breathing heavily. Anxiety rising. The walls closing in with each new thought. And a room emptier with every tick of the clock. This, again, was familiar territory.

The more pages I turned, the more I recognized her as a person. Seeing her as someone like me was somehow better and worse than seeing her as a role model. "Yep," I thought, "she's just as flawed and messed up as the rest of us." A follow-up question rolled through my mind: "Then where do all these good things I see so clearly in her come from?" I already knew the answer. I only needed a reminder: When you have access to everything, it's easy to fill the void.

She was turning to God, allowing Him to fill the void, then giving the everything away to others. And repeating the process—turning, receiving, giving. And again—turning, receiving, giving. If you want to capture this pattern poetically, you might write:

Here I am to give me back to you.
All I am, I am because of you.
Here I am.

"That's what I'm seeing," I thought, "God's love filtering through her." Shimmering, shining through her hurt. Dancing into her uncertainty. Love reflecting through a person—a broken person. "If He makes Himself known through a broken Jenny, He makes Himself known through a broken Sara," I reasoned. And it meant one beautiful thing. I could be myself—flaws and all—and God would use it. So I decided to be someone: me.

In 2017, Jenny visited Chicago for a solo-concert in the US. She spent time meeting fans during a special pre-show gathering created by Jessi and Anja. After the meet & greet, I was invited backstage to record a video clip for The Jenny Source. Jenny and I recorded the clip and chatted for a few minutes before we hugged and said our goodbyes.

And that's when she said something unexpected yet warmly welcomed. She spoke with genuine sincerity, although she couldn't possibly know the full depth of her own statement.

Those words—containing a quiet reflection of truth—hit the air and drifted gently into place. She looked squarely at me, paused, and said, "Thank you for being you."

"What's that red button?" Sara joking around in mid-flight with Chris, her only slightly amused pilot/brother (2017)

ABOUT THE AUTHOR: Sara lives in Houston, Texas, USA. You will find her putting her introversion to good use as a librarian at a local public library. She still loves a good adventure and new experiences, which is why her suitcase and passport are always within reach—and why there's a unicycle currently sitting in her garage. She loves listening to music and has been singing along badly, but joyfully, with Jenny's music since the summer of 1994. Her favorite official track is "Give Me The Faith" and her favorite unreleased track is "Always Welcome Here."

A Song Can Save a Life

by Carlos Arevalo

I have been a fan of Ace of Base since 1995 when I first heard "Beautiful Life" on the radio. And luckily, they sold the singles in the Chilean record stores. I bought *The Bridge* on cassette and I loved all the songs. Then the CD came out with the lyrics to the songs, and that was even better.

In the summer of 1996, Ace of Base came to Chile to play a concert at the *Viña del Mar* festival, but I was in the south of Chile on vacation with my family, so I could not see them live. I recorded the radio broadcast on cassette and recorded it on video when it was shown on television. That's when I fell in love with the voices of Jenny and Linn even more. I listened to the cassette and watched the video until they broke! In those times, there was no YouTube, so it was difficult to find that material (but not impossible), because many people recorded the *Viña del Mar* concerts.

I did not know any other Acer, nor did I know of fan clubs or anything like that. I thought I was the only fan in Chile. I only knew there were so many singles and discs, and versions of records and versions of songs.

In 1998, *Cruel Summer* arrived and I bought the single, the cassette, and the CD immediately! The internet was within everyone's reach, so I started to investigate what was happening with Linn because she was blurred in the photos, and because she did not sing so much in the songs anymore.

Then, thanks to the internet, I met two Chilean Acers who introduced me to other Acers and involved me in the world of Ace of Base. They had videos I did not have, songs I had no idea existed, photos I had never seen, etc. We met several times to share things and I started importing singles, albums, vinyl—all those things that were not imported or sold in Chile because it is so far away (and because it is a small country). All this continued until the band released their *Greatest Hits/Singles of the '90s* album. After "C'est La Vie," Ace of Base disappeared from the Chilean musical map.

In the year 2000, I stopped following the band due to my changes in style, music, etc. I started listening to other genres: punk, rock, hip-hop. When I stopped listening to the band, I started to live a more complicated life. All this process of change, I think, was generated because I entered the university. In 2002, I began studying Computer Engineering and I started to take part in social activities like helping poor children, abused women, the homeless, etc. I also started to listen to "Trova" music.

Then I went to Colombia for an internship at the university, and that's where I met a Cuban student. I fell in love with her, so I did everything possible to move to her country to finish my studies. In Cuba, my relationship with this girl was terminated. From there I stayed on the island to finish my studies.

In 2010, I fell into a worrisome depression. I had my first homosexual experience and it generated chaos within me since I began to recognize my sexuality. And in Latin America (as in some parts of the world), it is not well regarded. I did not know how to face future issues like the reaction of my parents, my brothers and sister, or my friends. Seeing how people treated homosexuals... I tried to have other relationships with women. However, I was attracted to my same sex over and over again.

I did not eat, I isolated myself from the people around me, and I fell into alcohol and drugs in that process. I stopped going to my university classes and I had drinks. I started to get together with the class bums and, with them, I started to use hard drugs. I became very thin and only went out to party, to drink, and to drug myself.

My entire study group and my trusted friends began to move away from me since everything I did was negative. I was also a bad example. (It was not good to be next to someone who was always high and smelled like alcohol.) In this way, I was totally alone. I begged for money to go shopping for my vices. I did not know who to talk to and I did not have the confidence to tell someone everything that was happening to me. It was the worst experience I could have had. It was so bad that I lost an entire year of study. And I was about to return to my country without finishing my studies.

On an afternoon in October of that year, I was on my way to buy alcohol and I passed by a pirate music store in La Havana. They had an angelic voice singing through their speakers—a voice I knew. I was hypnotized with a song I had never heard before. I went into the store and asked which song was the one that came from the speakers. To my surprise, the salesman showed me the solo music record of Jenny Berggren (a pirated bootleg). Without thinking twice, instead of using my money to buy alcohol, I bought the CD instead. I never thought Jenny Berggren of Ace of Base was singing solo.

I went back to my room and started looking for the song I had heard on my way. It was "Give Me The Faith." I had no idea what the song was about. I tried to find the lyrics on the internet and I realized it was a song towards God. I must confess that I am not a believer, however, upon discovering the meaning of the lyrics of the song, it caused a resounding change in me. The lyrics of the song gave me so much strength, so much harmony, so much clarity that it was able to change my way of seeing life. I do not believe in angels, but somehow I was at the right time and place where I heard an angel sing.

Since that afternoon, everything improved in an inexplicable way. The rector of the Cuban university approached me and helped me escape my depression. He accompanied me to the doctor and we began detoxification. He convinced me not to return to Chile until I finished my studies in Cuba. The whole detoxification was a difficult process, but I had the music of Jenny that gave me a lot of strength. My friends started visiting me again. When I left the clinic, I began to study with all my strength. Although I lost a year of study, I graduated with honors in 2011. That same year, I returned to Chile and started working in an important job.

I was able to talk with my family about my homosexuality, although it was not an easy process. Today, they already understand it. I met my partner David, of whom I am very much in love, and we have lived a beautiful life, like the song of which I became a fan of Ace of Base. Today I have my house, my car, my partner, and my life fully centered. I have not used alcohol and drugs again—and I will never do it again.

I am sure that without that episode, without discovering Jenny on my way, without having understood the message of the song, maybe my person would not exist today. That song saved my life.

Today, I am once again a fan of Ace of Base and, of course, Jenny Berggren (forever and always). I have a giant collection of Ace of Base albums and, of course, I have Jenny's original album and single, as well as her book (second edition), a shirt, and the *Så Mycket Bättre 2015* album.

I was so lucky to see her in concert last year in Peru. After the concert, there was a meet & greet. I brought two giant chocolates to give her plus my records to sign (there were too many), but when Jenny entered the area, it was chaos. I was lucky to be next to her when she entered. I was able to give her the chocolates, and it was at that moment that I could say to her, "Thank you, thank you very much for saving my life." Of course, she looked at me with curiosity, then she caressed my face and kissed my cheek. Then she signed ALL the discs that I brought. They are my greatest treasure.

Today I believe in light, in magic, and—above all—in angels.

Carlos meeting Jenny for the first time in Peru (2017)

ABOUT THE AUTHOR: Carlos lives in Santiago, Chile. Born in 1983, he is a civil engineer in computer science and an actor in a theater company in Santiago. He is always singing or playing video games in his free time. He loves animals and loves to travel a lot. He has been a fan of Ace of Base and Jenny's music since 1995, and his favorite unreleased track is "Let You In."

Breathing Air of Love That Comes to Us from Above

by Jessi Dieckow

"One step hesitation, one step into the night." I stand on the shores of Hovåsbadet, a place close to where I live. It is a Swedish beach with stony cliffs, and a deck where children jump from into the water during summer, just as in the Astrid Lindgren movies. I hear the seagulls scream and the waves of the water break at the shores. It is autumn 2000. I'm far away from home, all alone. I have my headphones in my ears and the volume up.

"Don't mind the weather it's raining in my heart tonight." Yeah, that is what I feel. I left everything behind me: my country, my family, my everything. I have been to Sweden before, all alone for holidays, but this time I'm here to stay longer... First for two years, maybe forever.

"I'm standing here in my ravine." I'm in my favorite country. This is everything I ever dreamt of, and yet, I feel lonely... I feel lost. Besides the family I'm staying with, I don't know a single person in this city. In that very moment, I doubt I made the right decision.

"Was a flower, so frail." How could it happen that I, the shyest person on earth, thinks she could live in a different country? A country with a language she barely understands? My doubts were as big as my dreams when I packed my suitcases some weeks back.

"The only place where you are near." And yet, there has to be a reason I ended up here. Nothing happens without a reason. I know this because when I look back on my life, I can see a red line that proves nothing happens without a reason. Yet, I have no clue where this will take me. "God, please help me to find my way," I beg as I stand on these shores, overwhelmed by the surroundings and my feelings. The music from my favorite band still plays in my headphones. Like a dramatic backing soundtrack, narrating my journey into the unknown. I notice the sun is starting to set, so I go back to the place I now call home.

* * *

I'm around eight-years-old when I have my first encounter with God. I live in the former German Democratic Republic. Far away from the western world, far away from Coca-Cola, McDonald's, and *Bravo* magazines.

Going to church is not popular. Serving the party and the system is better. I was not allowed to be baptised as a baby, my mother tells me. My father was in the party, so being a member of the church at the same time was not allowed. And even if my parents were divorced several years by that time, and so getting baptised would not have any effect, my mom didn't get that done afterwards.

But I have a friend who is active in church. She goes to a playgroup there, so I go with her. And I have so much fun. I hear interesting stories from a book called the Bible, we draw pictures about these stories, and sing songs. And I love stories, drawing, and singing. I just love the time there. But somehow, at the same time, I have the feeling I do something wrong. It's like going into the forest when you are forbidden to do so. Going to church was something I had never done and thought it wouldn't be ok.

When I get home again, I tell my mom where I had been. I ask her if it was wrong. She smiles at me and says, "There is nothing wrong with going to church if you want to. If God is reaching out for you, take this hand." Being eight years old, I barely understand what she is talking about. I had never been to a church before. I had no idea what happens there and I don't think much about it in the time after. I don't even remember if I visited the Christian playgroup several times or if that single time is stuck in my head.

Some time later, my whole life changes when I experience the edge of the 'Ravine' for the first time. And not only because the wall between East and West Germany is knocked down. We from the eastern part suddenly can buy Coca-Cola, I have my first hamburger, and I get my very first *Bravo* magazine—all for a fortune. But also because my beloved grandmother dies after a dreadful time of sickness when I'm nine years old. She is living with us, and is always the second half of what I mean when I talk about my parents. It happens several times that I find my mom in tears. I ask her what is wrong, but she cannot tell me the truth.

Another part of my parents is my grandfather. He is living in Heaven, that I know for sure. He is sitting on his cloud, looking down at me and taking care of me. He died three months before I was born, but in my nine-year-old life, he is as present as the rest of my wonderful family. He is just not visible. And that is ok. I know that he is there and has always been as my guardian angel.

"I'm standing here in my ravine." That day, I wake up in the morning and go over to the living room where my grandmother is laying. My mom is sitting next to her bed. "Grandmommy is asleep forever," Mom tells me, and my little world is tumbling down. I understand the meaning of that and yet I don't.

Mom lights a candle and I sit next to her. She takes my hand in hers and says, "Let us pray." I have never prayed before in my whole life but I haven't lost someone in my whole life before either. My mom starts praying the Lord's Prayer. I open my mouth and pray with her as if it is the most natural thing I would do. I have never heard any prayer before and I don't know why, but the words come right from my heart. They just flow out of my mouth.

Only a few people have telephones by that time, so my mom has to go to a neighbour at the end of the street to get a doctor. And I stay there. I'm not afraid; I feel that I'm surrounded by love; by a power I cannot grasp.

"The only place on earth where [he is] near." From this time on, we are going to church. Not very often, but every now and then. When I'm eleven, my mom signs me up for confirmation class. She tells me that my grandmommy always wanted me to get baptised and to get to know about God. So I go there. The girl who took me to the playgroup when I was eight is in that class too. Now that the wall is gone and Germany is reunited, people are allowed to openly believe in God and go to church, so I enjoy the afternoons there.

* * *

Not many years later, I have my first encounter with a band called Ace of Base. I love their music, have my first crush on Ulf Ekberg, and admire the lead singer Malin Berggren. My whole room has posters everywhere. I have changed to high school and try to fit in there somehow. My best friend at that time likes my fave band too. Just as many others play being the band, my friend and I do too. Since my friend is blonde and I have brown hair, I end up as Jenny. Because I have had rather a tomboy style before, my mom is happy when I finally change my style because of that band I'm admiring. *'Here I am,'* I finally start to dress like a girl.

281

In Germany, we have practical classes in school where students spend two weeks with a real job; you have to do a presentation afterwards and talk about your work there. I want to become a journalist and I'm writing all the time. And I love, love, love languages, so I'm doing my training the first year at a newspaper. In the second year, my first choice is to work in a record company, but I'm denied. So I choose my other interest and work in a church instead, which feels more natural.

"You'll be living in danger." 1994 is the year I hear the band live for the first time. I live in Berlin and the very first "European Music Awards" are hosted in town. Berlin is the perfect place, the symbol for the connection of the western with the eastern world. My mom takes me out of school that day and we go there early. When we arrive, we hear "Living In Danger" from afar. They are having their soundcheck.

This is the first time I see my favorite band not on TV only. It is the end of November and it is freezing cold. Being fourteen years old, temperatures don't matter. I have my Ace of Base shirt and a thin leather jacket and I'm freezing my ass off. The location is well protected, so we have no chance to get close (times have changed since then). We see all the celebrities arrive in big buses and taxis in the evening. All in all, we spend almost a whole day there. We hear the soundcheck of "Living in Danger," and later, the live performance from afar. When the show is over and I sit in the train, I can barely bend my legs because I stood all day and the cold is in my whole body. I'm freezing all night.

Early the next morning, we go back to the hotel. I want to meet my favorite band so bad. We stand several hours before we find out that the band had left minutes before we arrived. No luck this time. But that day, my mom becomes a fan of the band. She finds it impressive that Ace of Base showed sympathy with their fans by playing outside while all the other artists sat in the cosy tent that was constructed behind the Brandenburg Gate. So they earn at least one fan this night.

"The Bridge To The Base." In early 1995, I find out that the former Official German Fan Club doesn't exist anymore. So I write to the record company in Germany and apply to run the fan club. I tell them I want to do all the work, from creating fan magazines to sending out autographs. This was my biggest dream at that time. I could do all the things I love, support my favorite band, and I can write. I get the refusal some months later. Understandable from today's perspective, but back then, some part of my world broke. But I didn't give up. If I cannot be official, I can still do it. I can be unofficial. *The Bridge* is my favorite album, so my mom suggests "The Bridge To The Base" for the fan club and the magazine, and so it is set.

My mom is my biggest supporter through all my crazy Ace of Base projects. She was, and still is, always backing me up. No idea I have is too silly and she never attempts to block my fandom. I also have a lot of pen pals by that time. Over fifty Acers—as we fans call ourselves—from all around the world. So writing takes up a lot of my teenage time. Writing articles for the fan mag, writing letters to my pen pals, writing lyrics for songs, writing poems, writing stories. Besides singing, writing is my life.

I am baptised the same day I am confirmed. My first name Jessica means "God is watching." Being confirmed, I get the line, "I will bless you and make your name great, so that you will be a blessing" to live by as part of the ritual. In our church, you could chose a line from the Bible yourself, but I left that to our priest. I don't want to take a line out of the Bible and make it to my own.

When I am sixteen, I travel to Gothenburg for the first time. It is only one week, but I enjoy it so much. I always wanted to go there just to see all the places that have influenced the people I admire the most, and to see what inspires them to write the music of my life is a dream come true. Even if it is only a week in October (and raining a lot), I have the time of my life.

"Have you heard, have your heard?" During the *World Music Awards* in 1997, I recognize Jenny for the first time as the outstanding person she is. The show is only available on pay-TV in Germany, so I'm sitting in front of the TV, watching that blurry, encoded black-and-white screen. I can barely see anything. Then Ace of Base is announced and I get excited, but instead of Malin, Jenny enters the stage singing one of my all-time-favorite songs, "Ravine." And all I can think is, *"She looks like an angel."* I can only see the silhouette, and since the signal is encoded, it looks like she is wearing a white dress. I'm pretty disappointed some days later when I finally see that performance decoded and realize that the dress was yellow. On the other hand, it feels like I just saw her soul the other day. Sometimes the blurriness makes you see things clear. So, this first impression is stuck in my mind. Of course, I know that Ace of Base consists of four people, but until that day, Jenny seemed to always be the funny, joking second singer from the back while her sister was standing in the limelight.

In 1999, there are rumours that the band is going to split because Malin wants to open a tanning studio. I call the record company and find out that the dad of the Berggrens has just passed away and that this is the reason they have cancelled some shows. My mom and I are busy comforting Acers who call me and are totally devastated; some even want to commit suicide. We spend several hours telling them that this is only a rumour and that there are other reasons for the postponed appointments.

"To the Moon and Back." The same year, on my nineteenth birthday, I go to Gothenburg on my own for the first time (My mom would come up one week later). When I arrive, I meet up with some of my pen pals from Germany who are also there and we have a little celebration. They tell me that Jenny is going to play at a festival the week after in a nearby town. It is a church festival and I'm looking so much forward to finally seeing her live.

It becomes the first time I meet Jenny in person. It occurs some weeks after her father's death and she seems very fragile. Yet she is so kind and takes more time than I ever imagined. I don't remember much from the meeting. Being the worst small talker ever, I can barely say anything. My mom and Jenny do most of the talking, and I'm so touched by Jenny's kindness. And I'm the luckiest person when I hand over one of the fan magazines from my fan club and Jenny tells me that she knows them since I used to send every issue over to Sweden.

Only one year later, I'm back in my favorite town on earth. I have graduated from school, and since I can not decide what I want to do with the rest of my life, I decide that I want to live in Sweden for two years. I want to learn the language fluently—that is the goal when I head north in August 2000.

"In the dark I found a way to a friend." So all alone—in this new surrounding in the foreign country—my first way leads me to church. I try all different churches in Gothenburg. And I end up in a small cosy church where I attend services regularly from the first time I go there. This is the only place I feel at home.

"The only place on earth where [he is] near." I join their choir since (as you know) I just love to sing, and what is the best way to learn a new language? Practice!

I go to the church store at Smyrnakyrkan in central Gothenburg and buy a pin that states "What would Jesus do?" Funny enough, this pin is simply a cross with the letters wwjd, which is partly my initials. Spending so much time in churches, singing psalms, and taking part in services, I experience my belief in a totally different way than ever before. Suddenly my journey makes sense. I realize it one day while writing in my diary in the evening. I'm not here because my favorite band comes from this town; no, I'm meant to be here to deepen my connection to God. To study not only Swedish, but also to be filled with God's love.

First, I have hard times at the first family. I try my best to melt in. The kids love me, their parents tell me I'm doing fine, and I start to feel at home. At Christmas, my mom comes over to celebrate with me. I don't want to have any presents. Being with my family is the only thing I need ... and snow. So at one of the services I go to almost every Sunday, I tell God: "All I want for Christmas is my mom and a beautiful celebration."

At that time, I have no idea how seldom snow is, even in Gothenburg. I think, "If I'm in Sweden, I need snow for Christmas." There is no snow when I go to the midnight service on Christmas Eve and I'm a little disappointed, though I enjoy the Christmas songs we sing with the choir. When the service is over, I get out of church and realize that some snowflakes are dancing in the air. And when I look up, I realize that those are the biggest snowflakes I have ever seen. This is the second best Christmas present ever, besides being with family.

Every now and then, I go to one of Jenny's rare church performances. I just sit there and listen to the beautiful music. I never have the guts to go and speak to her afterwards. It feels like disturbing her privacy, so I just enjoy the peace inside me that her music brings.

Some months later, the family tells me they cannot have me anymore. I find out that they never registered me correctly and working as an au pair is not allowed—even with their permission. From one day to the other, they tell me I have to leave. During summer, I look for a new family, find one, and move to this family. They are nice; I get along well with the kids. My Swedish has improved big time because of the great practice I have in the choir. But this family also ends our contract long before we had agreed. And suddenly, I find myself on the way back to Germany.

It seems I'm back on track one. No idea what to do with my future. My plan to study in Sweden fails big time, so I need to find an education in Germany. Looking back, having to leave Sweden early has saved me a year with nothing to do. Right when I'm back, I start to apply for different apprentices and finally find one in fall 2002. Only some weeks later, I go to my very first Acer Meeting. And there, I meet one of my two lifetime friends—Anja. Right from the start, we start talking and cannot stop. One of the things I would definitely miss if it wasn't for Ace of Base.

She tells me about her work she does for the former 4-ever website as an ambassador (as the helping people are called there) and I tell her about my fan club, which I've run six years by that time. Acer meetings are happening regularly in Germany at that time, so we see each other at every meeting and become good friends.

When I'm back from the International Acer Meeting in 2003 where I met many international Acers I only knew from letters, I tell her how great it was and encourage her to come with me the year after. So we go to the International Acer Meeting 2004 together.

During this Acer Meeting, I meet Jenny for the second and third time. Together with all the Acers, we go to Hunnebostrand. We almost missed that opportunity because we were staying at the home of two French Acers. We had just arrived at the hostel that day when someone told us that we would go to a Jenny concert in the evening. So we turn around and go back to the place we're staying because ever since I met Jenny at the church festival in 1999, I felt the need to give her the videotape of that performance. I have the feeling that this performance was special for her; certainly due to another reason as for me, but still I have that feeling that she needs to have this tape.

So we head back to Angered, which is pretty far outside Gothenburg. We run the whole time between the trams and their home. We grab our stuff and go back to the hostel just in time for departure. After the performance, we all get to talk a little bit with her. I hand over my videotape and I'm so excited that I have no idea what we talked about. We meet her again one week later with only a handful of Acers at another church concert, which I enjoy so much. I learn that it is ok to talk to her after her church performances.

Anja and I talk about starting our own website. Anja has the programming skills and I have tons of ideas in my head. Fan magazines seem almost outdated; although I hold onto them for another year. The web provider we want to use has a special offer for Easter if you have "ei" in your name, which means egg in German. So after a lot of playing around with words, I come up with the name "Aceisland." We get our special offer and another part of the history has started.

One year later, the big Ace of Base revival happens. Something no Acer ever expected. Ace of Base are going to Antwerp and, of course, we are joining. Meet & greets are happening after the show. We see Jenny, Ulf, and Jonas on the streets of Antwerp. But we never dare walk up to them (except for the official meetings) since Jenny has her little baby son with her. And we don't want to disturb that privacy.

Our website is growing, my skills to fill the sites are developing, and we both work well as a team. Each of us brings a package of other visions and skills that enriches the combination and, while other websites come and go, we remain and become a stable part of the Acer community.

Since Jenny is the most active member of the band, we soon discover that we have the most content about her. So we discuss moving Jenny's side projects to a separate platform as a part of the Aceisland website. In the beginning, it is called "Just another piece of Aceisland" referring to the line in "Wave Wet Sand." Taking care of the public relations, I post the link everywhere with the line "Your Source to the activities of Jenny Berggren." Soon it becomes shorter and The Jenny Source was born. In 2007, we register our own domain for this part of Aceisland since the content takes up too much space on our server.

The same year, in November, we head to Copenhagen to another Ace of Base concert where I would meet a lot of dear Acer friends again. After the show, a meet & greet is organized again and when I walk up to Jenny, she looks at me and says, "I don't know your first name but your last name is Dieckow." I'm like "Wow!" Not only because she is one of the very few people who pronounces it correctly, but also because she just keeps me speechless. I wasn't expecting that at all.

Ace of Base are doing more concerts from that time on and the money I put down on CDs in the past is now spent on travel to different Ace of Base concerts. And if there are no Ace of Base concerts, we travel to Sweden to see Jenny's church concerts, which mean more and more to me the more often I go. And even though I totally enjoy the Ace of Base concerts of the Redefined Tour, nothing beats the church concerts she does. It always feels like coming home. A feeling I cannot explain because words are not enough.

Swedish churches give me a different feeling than German ones. I feel even closer to God then, just like coming home. Maybe because it is more common in Sweden to go to church, more accepted. In Germany—at least in the part I live in—I always get looks when I talk about my belief. In Sweden, it is no big deal. Sweden itself has become my calm point. Every time I go there, it feels like I'm going on a trip to a pilgrimage. As soon as I enter Swedish ground, all my senses are being zeroed. I get calm, it feels like an ongoing meditation. I speak a lot to God, think about things that are important to me, discuss problems with him that need to be solved. Definitely something I'm doing far too seldom at home in Germany.

Our Jenny website is becoming more and more popular and recognized. We even get messages from Swedish churches that want to book her. I forward every single message to her booking agency for church concerts and breakfast sessions. It is fun to help out.

Jenny starts to travel the world and Acers ask us if there is a chance to meet her. I organise the first meet & greets in different parts of the world: Canada, Mexico, Spain, the United States, Russia, and Germany. It is fun, and also in the middle of the night when meetings happen on the other side of the world as I'm sitting awake trying to coordinate and bring the right people together. Seeing all the happy Acers in pictures and hearing their excitement, reading how happy they are, and helping them realise how important love and concern for one another is...This is definitely one of the best parts in my journey so far.

"[I was]lost now [I'm] found by the love, by the light." And finally, my journey makes sense, even though I needed quite some time to realize it. God was reaching out for me my whole life, but I needed Jenny to help me realize my deep connection to God—and what he is able to do and accomplish. How easy it is to let him into your heart, how easy it is to believe, and how much pressure he can take away from the everyday life.

On the other hand, finding that connection made me find Jenny as the great, warm, good-hearted person she is—and I admire that. She has always been my role model, even if I didn't know that from the beginning when I would have rather played her sister while doing playback to Ace of Base's music.

Nowadays I consider her a friend. I don't have many people I call a friend because I have a hard time trusting people and opening myself up. To be honest, only six people took that hurdle and she is, along with Anja and Sara, definitely one of them. For every single one of them, I would go to the moon and back to make sure they are fine and I would give them the shirt off my back if needed. And all of my six friends I have, I have because of Ace of Base.

The times are gone when I stood in front of her and didn't know what to say because I'm so overwhelmed to stand in front of my idol. It's not Jenny from Ace of Base I have in front of me but a person who respects me for who I am, whose trust I have earned over the past twenty years as much as she has earned mine.

Now I'm happy to meet her and help her to get in touch with her fanbase. I have fun taking pictures for all the Acers around the world that cannot make it. I'm happy to build bridges for the Acers by taking them to venues on the other side of the world, sharing pictures, videos, and information.

I am filled with satisfaction to know how happy Jenny is to meet all you lovely fans around the world and to know how happy you Acers are to finally be able to tell her your stories face to face—and letting her know how much she helped you on your life journey after so many years. Sometimes I wonder where I would be now if I had not been found by *"the love, by the light"* that Jenny's journey has brought for me.

I know that my story is only one of many about how much impact this Swedish girl, now grown woman, has had on everyone's life. Each story is touching, and a proof of the beauty she has brought to all our lives.

Even though it has been a long journey (and a long story in this book), looking back on my life and the things I experienced—the good, and the bad, and the dreadful—it all happened for a reason and there was, is, and will always be air of love that comes to me right from above.

Jessi and Jenny working through an autograph request list

Jenny live on stage in Schwäbisch Gmünd, Germany (2017)

Jenny and Jakob live on stage in Oberhausen, Germany (2017)

Afterword

Nearly forty stories of inspiration from fans in twenty countries: Belarus, Brazil, Chile, Estonia, Germany, Hungary, Indonesia, Israel, Latvia, Mexico, the Netherlands, Peru, Poland, Portugal, Russia, Scotland, Spain, the United States, Uzbekistan, and Venezuela. Together, their stories showcase the impact a musician can create through song. And together, they represent a mere sample of the tales that can be told.

But do these stories answer the "what" and the "how" of that original question? Do they show the outcome of Jenny's lyrical prayer in "Give Me The Faith"? Reading these stories, I hear the answer as a silent song singing its way through each page. A song of grace sweeping through each life.

This particular song of grace first gained momentum through a band called Ace of Base and it continues moving through Jenny's solo work today—producing fruit like friendship, love, hope, kindness, joy, optimism, and oh-so-much-more in the lives of listeners everywhere.

All this abundant grace flows freely because one woman, her siblings, and a friend decided to team up and share their talent through song. That band and its music is now a part of history. Ace of Base's legacy sings us forward in recorded form. Meanwhile, Jenny continues her work as a conduit for grace—singing and speaking words of joy as she travels from one city to the next.

You might think this song of grace, this type of influence is reserved for people with an established platform in the world. The truth is, we all have the same ability to be a conduit; to influence others with the talent, gifts, and lives we possess. When you choose to become a conduit, you create stories like these—and they are written in the minds and hearts of people around you.

By supporting this book, you have made a difference for the children in Voi. This type of impact adds up. Multiply such small, medium, and large impacts by your days and it means you are making a dramatic difference too.

Most of us will never command the same massive audience as an artist of Jenny's caliber. But such a supersized scale is not necessary to make a difference in the lives of one another.

One day, maybe tomorrow, another person will turn to you and ask you to speak them forward or heal them forward or write them forward or move them forward. And when you do, when you love another person forward, you become a natural superstar—the best kind of superstar imaginable.

—Sara, on behalf of The Jenny Source

About the Author

The Jenny Source started in 2006 as a category within Aceisland, an Ace of Base fan site run by Anja Mummhardt and Jessi Dieckow. By that time, Jenny had cultivated many projects of her own alongside Ace of Base, so Anja and Jessi thought it best to devote a larger part of the site to Jenny's solo projects.

In less than a year, the side category proved too small for the content, so they allocated yet more space within the main site. Still, the content overflowed. So they created a stand-alone site dedicated to Jenny's solo work and registered the current domain in May 2007.

For more than a decade, Anja and Jessi have cultivated a treasure trove of information on Jenny and her music by documenting concerts, organizing meet & greets, and conducting one-on-one interviews. It has become a well-known and well-respected site within the fan community.

Do you have comments about this book or The Jenny Source? Email us at info@jennyberggren.net or contact the team at the links below.

You can connect with me on:
- http://www.jennyberggren.net
- https://www.facebook.com/thejennysource
- https://www.instagram.com/thejennysource
- https://www.youtube.com/user/thejennysource

Printed in Great
Britain
by Amazon

31092101R00184